BOB MARLEY...

BOB MARLEY...

HERE ARE **OVER 200** BANDS, CDS, FILMS, AND OTHER ODDITIES THAT YOU WILL LOVE

DAVE THOMPSON

AN IMPRINT OF HAL LEONARD CORPORATION

Published in 2013 by Backbeat Books
An Imprint of Hal Leonard Corporation
7777 West Bluemound Road
Milwaukee, WI 53213

Trade Book Division Editorial Offices
33 Plymouth St., Montclair, NJ 07042

Printed in the United States of America

Book design by Michael Kellner

Library of Congress Cataloging-in-Publication Data

Thompson, Dave, 1960 January 3-
If you like Bob Marley... here are over 200 bands, CDs, films, and other oddities that you will love / by Dave Thompson.
pages cm
Includes bibliographical references and index.
ISBN 978-1-4768-8681-7 (alk. paper)
1. Reggae music--History and criticism. 2. Reggae music--Miscellanea.
3. Marley, Bob. I. Title.
ML3532.T56 2013
781.646--dc23

2013001234

www.backbeatbooks.com

To Tim Cross,
who rarely needed to guess who was coming to dinner

CONTENTS

IF YOU
LIKE
BOB
MARLEY...

Bob Marley and the Wailers, poised and purposeful. (Photofest)

Introduction

When reggae first raised its head in the world of rock 'n' roll, a lot of people laughed.

Rock 'n' roll people, anyway.

Like the loudmouthed, spotty kid in the schoolyard of our past, rock, in its youth, was a sanctimonious little beast. On the one hand, it was so consumed with insecure self-belief that it was forever trying to "better" itself by hanging out with the posh kids . . . orchestras, opera lovers, playwrights, and so on. But on the other, it thought nothing about crudely hurling juvenile insults at anyone it perceived could be teased for cheap laughs: disco fans, teenyboppers, crooners. And, oddly for such an international language, anybody unfortunate enough to have been born outside of the Anglo-American universe.

It was not a xenophobic dislike; or, at least, it was not knowingly so. Prior to the mid-1980s, you could count on one hand the number of truly successful ethnic rock 'n' roll performers, particularly those who could not also be lumped into some other generic bag as well.

World music was still a marketing opportunity waiting to happen, and the nature of the music industry in general ensured that even performers from mainland Europe were unlikely to get a fair share of the commercial stick in America. Move farther afield, to Latin America, or even Japan and Australia, and you might as well grab your coat and turn the lights out behind you. The fact that most readers of a certain age can still remember the names of every exception to that rule (Golden Earring, Focus, Kraftwerk, and the Sadistic Mika Band) is evidence enough of that.

So, when elements of both the American and British music press started to champion Bob Marley and the Wailers in the early to mid-1970s, most hardcore rock fans took one look at the press release . . . a Jamaican-born Rastafarian who played reggae music . . . and switched off on the spot. Because reggae, in the 1970s, wasn't simply the kid in the corner who got bullied by his playmates every single day. The teachers and school governors picked on it as well.

It all sounds the same.

It doesn't have a tune.

It doesn't have good words (and you couldn't understand them if it did).

It isn't really music.

It wasn't simply a different world back then. It was a different planet; and if you don't believe me, ask Chris Blackwell, whose Island Records released Bob Marley and the Wailers' *Catch a Fire* LP in 1973. Keyboard player John "Rabbit" Bundrick of Free, and Muscle Shoals guitarist Wayne Perkins, were drafted in to add rocking overdubs to the finished disc simply to make the record sound more accessible to rock audiences.

Almost four decades on from Marley's commercial breakthrough—thirty-plus years on from his death and nearly two decades after his induction into the Rock and Roll Hall of Fame—that task, too, seems like a relic from a different age. So does the argument, loudly raised in the music press of the day, that Marley himself had little to do with his own popularity; that it was Eric Clapton, scoring a massive hit with the Wailers' "I Shot the Sheriff," who first pushed his boat out into the commercial mainstream. Which is kind of true, and our first chapter will explore that happenstance in detail. But Clapton had hits with a lot of other people's music too, and when was the last time you saw a J. J. Cale poster on sale in Wal-Mart?

Today, it seems as though no discussion of modern music can pass without reference to Bob Marley's influence; no examination of its political significance can be considered without his mention; and no visit to the local record store can be complete without a quick glance up the reggae aisle to see how many more dubious compilations of oft-recycled oldies have hit the streets since last time.

During his own lifetime, Bob Marley released just twelve "new" albums, plus one dub set and two live collections. Of these, four—1965's Jamaica-only ***The Wailin' Wailers***, 1970's oddly titled ***The Best of the Wailers*** and ***Soul Rebel***, and 1972's ***Soul Revolution***—predate the band's arrival at Island Records; three spanned the period while the band awaited success (***Catch a Fire***, ***Burnin'***, and ***Natty Dread***); the remainder (***Rastaman Vibration***, ***Exodus***, ***Kaya***, ***Survival***, and ***Uprising***) followed fame. And all have been reissued and repackaged more times than maybe seems prudent. But no matter how shoddily packaged the latest collection of oldies and outtakes might be, the sheer quality of Marley and the Wailers' music always shines through.

It shines, too, through the manifold interpretations of his music that have percolated into western consciousness in the decades since **Johnny Nash** gave him his first-ever taste of international fame with a cover of "Stir It Up" in 1972. From **Joe Strummer**'s fragile reinvention of "Redemption Song" to **Sinead O'Connor**'s *Saturday Night Live*–inflaming delivery of "War"; from the Fugees' "No Woman, No Cry" to Annie Lennox's plaintive "Waiting in Vain," Marley is now one of the most-covered songwriters of the rock 'n' roll era. And, once again, one of the most respected, a process that culminated with Marley's recognition by the Rock and Roll Hall of Fame in 1994, but that peaked, perhaps, with his induction into the Songwriters Hall of Fame in 2010.

That is how far reggae has come since Marley's breakthrough. Today, nobody knocks reggae for its perceived lack of musical quality, lyrical depth, or political impact—not with songs the strength of . . . well, all of the above, but many more, too . . . ranged against them; and nobody knocks Bob Marley, either.

Of course, we still have a long way to go, at least if the Rock and Roll Hall of Fame is the yardstick by which we judge things. Chris Blackwell was inducted in 2001 for services that included (but were by no means limited to) his tireless work to popularize reggae during its years on the outside; and **Jimmy Cliff**, too, has been recognized. But otherwise, Jamaica has not troubled the induction committee in the slightest.

How come? To argue that Marley and Cliff are the only reggae performers in over half a century to have made any impact on the overall music scene is as . . . well, name almost any other inductee you choose, but let's say the Police, who themselves started life as a reggae parody band . . . is as blinkered (at best) and blindly prejudiced (at worst) as the detractors who held the music down in the first place.

It was only fitting, however, that Marley should be the first to be included. Because without him, the music might still be a backwater cultural oddity whose cult appeal floats somewhere between the electric bouzouki and the bong guitar.

Which, in turn, means if you like Bob Marley, you are going to love a lot of other things.

A NOTE ABOUT SONG TITLES AND ARTISTS' NAMES

Quite conceivably, every song title in this book appears in different places with slight variations in spelling or punctuation. This is a consequence of so many versions being released and rereleased, recorded and rerecorded, across a span of years, by a variety of performers, in a land where correct accounting of titles and lyrics was deemed secondary to simply getting the record out.

Is it "54-46 Was My Number" or "54-46, That's My Number"? Is it "A Message to You Rudy" (with or without a comma) or "Rudy, A Message to You"? Is it "Satta Amasa Gana" or "Satta Massagana"? "Dem A fe Get a Beating" or "Them Ha fe Get a Beaten"? And so forth.

Less frequently, but noticeably still, artists' names can be equally problematic, and for many of the same reasons. Tappa Zukie or Tapper Zukie? Ansel Collins or Ansell . . . or even Ansil? Willi or Willie Williams? U Roy or Hugh Roy?

With this in mind—but always with at least one example at hand—I have chosen one version of a title or name, and stuck with it throughout. Alternate versions are too numerous to list in this book, but they may be found on the Internet.

AUTHOR'S NOTE

Throughout this book, certain names, titles, etc., are noted in boldface. This occurs only at the first, or primary reference to each, and indicates that the subject is considered worthy of further inspection.

Eric Clapton. He shot the sheriff and reggae never looked back.
(RSO Records/Photofest)

1

SHOOTING THE SHERIFF: ERIC CLAPTON AND THE BIRTH OF ROCKING REGGAE

Strange but true. For most listeners of a certain age, the first time they heard Bob Marley, they had Eric Clapton to thank for it.

In Jamaica, reggae music permeates life like nothing else. You are barely a page into author Kwame Dawes's "My Lord," the first of the short stories in the anthology *Kingston Noir*, and he speaks of it: "The sweet heaviness of heartbreak and desire, like a great Alton Ellis tune seeping out of a rum bar...the kind of tune that makes you want to cry and laugh, and screw, and hug-up, and pray at the same time."

Elsewhere, however...elsewhere, not so much. Until Eric Clapton came along.

The Guitarist Formerly Known as God had been through some hard times lately. The successive breakup of the supergroups Cream and Blind Faith had left him reeling; drug abuse and a shattered ego left him teetering. An attempt to hide behind anonymity in the oddly named Derek and the Dominos collapsed after one admittedly legendary album; and a first solo LP caught him in such a pensive state that even his beloved guitar seemed to be taking a vacation. He needed to rebuild and re-launch, but he needed to do it on his own terms. No harking back to past glories; no living off a meal ticket he had tired of years before.

So when he called manager Robert Stigwood, and told him to hire a studio and book a producer, all concerned were adamant that there should be no pressure on the reluctant superstar. Taking over Miami's Criteria Studios with producer Tom Dowd, from the moment Clapton arrived, things were kept low key. The studio had been booked for twenty-four hours a day, every day, meaning Clapton and the musicians who were slowly making their way into the building could play whenever the mood hit them (rather than try and squeeze inspiration into a few preset eight-hour sessions).

He drew in musicians from wherever they came. Drummer Carl Radle was a member of Clapton's Derek and the Dominos, and he made a few suggestions. So did Dowd, and so did other players who stopped by. But from our point of view, the key arrival was guitarist **George Terry**, whom Clapton first met during the Dominos sessions, and who had been hanging around ever since. Because it was Terry who brought along a tape of Bob Marley and the Wailers' recently released *Burnin'* album; and when Clapton fell in love with one song, "I Shot the Sheriff," the die was cast.

With Terry and vocalist **Yvonne Elliman** almost instantly coming up with a harmony line, and Clapton learning the words just as fast, the first producer Dowd knew of the song was when he heard them playing it live in the studio. The tapes rolled and, while there was still some way to go before the album (named for the studio's street address, ***461 Ocean Boulevard***) could be called complete, everybody knew they'd already created something special.

The song's slow-burning reggae rhythm was almost deceptive. It was a rock performance with a Jamaican beat, and that was maybe to its advantage. Other artists turning their hands to different musical styles at that time were usually accused of having "gone" somewhere—also in 1974, for instance, David Bowie would "go disco." The following year, **the Rolling Stones** purportedly drove in the same direction. But nobody ever accused Clapton of "going reggae," not even when the wonderful world of bootlegs unleashed a few other highlights from the Criteria sessions, including a solid seven-minute skank through "I Shot the Sheriff," and a deeply reggaefied version of the old Cream blues staple "Crossroads."

No, "I Shot the Sheriff" was simply a great song, in a great arrangement, and it became a great hit record.

It was not released into a vacuum. Reggae was already a well-known quantity in Britain, where ska and reggae records had been making the Top 10 for years now. But when they did so, it was often under the guise of a novelty song, high-octane dance music with grunt-and-shout propulsion and a wacky-baccy beat.

Records like **Nora Dean**'s "Barbed Wire," with its so-memorable chorus: "He got barbed wire in his underpants, oh mamaaaaaaaaaaaaaaaa!"; **Max Romeo**'s "Wet Dream," with its insistence that his girl lie down, "let me push it up, push it up"; or **Dave and Ansel Collins**'s British chart-topping "Double Barrel." "I am the magnificent!" declares vocalist **Dave Barker**. "I'm backed by the shack of a soul boss, most turnin', stormin' sound o' soul." Except not many people knew what the real lyrics were, so they made up their own and it sounded even better.

That was reggae music, then, for anyone who didn't know any better; or else it was Caribbeanized versions of top pop songs from the U.K. or the U.S.; or it was the swaying-palm-trees, summer sounds of singers like Johnny Nash, a Houston, Texas, born performer who was hitherto best known for discovering the Cowsills. Then in 1972, he scored an American chart-topper with the infectious "I Can See Clearly Now," and the following year challenged for honors again with the even more insidious "Stir It Up."

And who played on both songs, and actually penned the latter? Bob Marley and the Wailers. Although nobody knew that at the time; or if they did, they didn't care. Besides, no matter who was backing his smooth tones on wax, Nash coated his recordings with a polish and sheen through which the music's island origins were barely discernible.

Eric Clapton, on the other hand, embraced those origins with a passion, let his love for the sound shine through unabashedly, and consummated rock 'n' roll's unspoken love affair with reggae in a way that no other white rocker ever had.

He was a pioneer; but even more than that, he was a frustratingly modest one. Arguably, Clapton's recording of "I Shot the Sheriff" did more to break reggae into the rock mainstream than any other single event in the music's history. But the man himself refused to acknowledge his achievement. First, he claimed it would be self-indulgent to take the credit that other observers were willing to offer him; then he admitted that he hadn't actually wanted the track released in the first place. He furiously opposed Dowd's inclusion of it on the album, arguing that his rendition of the song was so inferior to Marley's original that it was almost an insult.

Dowd wouldn't budge, however. He'd been given *carte blanche* over *461 Ocean Boulevard*'s contents, and that was the way it was going to stay. Neither could Clapton rely on management for support. The moment he heard the track, manager Stigwood agreed wholeheartedly with Dowd, then rubbed salt into Clapton's wounds by announcing that it was going to be the first single as well.

Stigwood's RSO label was still a relatively new venture at that time; the company's first release, the Bee Gees' "Saw a New Morning" 45, had appeared little more than a year before, in March 1973, and the company was still awaiting its first major hit. But from the moment "I Shot the Sheriff" was unveiled, with its sparkling translation of what many people still considered an alien musical form, and a lyric that appealed on so many levels, the RSO sales team knew that their luck was about to change.

"I Shot the Sheriff" was released as a 45 in June 1974, just a couple of weeks ahead of the parent album. Three months later it reached #1, hitting the top in the same week as the *461 Ocean Boulevard* album slipped from the same pinnacle. RSO never looked back; and in terms of an American breakthrough, neither did reggae music. Within a year, the Wailers' own original version of the song was riding on the chart, as the *Burnin'* album made its own belated appearance in the Top 200.

APRÈS ERIC, *LE DÉLUGE:* TEN SERIOUSLY UNEXPECTED WHITE REGGAE SONGS

"Dreadlock Holiday"—10cc (1978)

A delightfully sunny pop-reggae backing accompanies this cautionary tale of a white man lost in the Jamaican backwaters; in more politically correct times, it would be very easy to be offended by the mock-patois voices that threaten the hapless tourist's well-being. And that is before you hit the trouble-soothing chorus of "I don't like cricket . . . I love it!" Because we all know that even the toughest ghetto gangster can be distracted by the clunk of ball on willow.

Fortunately, listeners in 1978 had more important things to worry about than imagined insults or latent British colonialism. For them, "Dreadlock Holiday" emerged as one of the most single-mindedly joyous stabs at white reggae ever conceived, a fitting successor to past 10cc hits "Rubber Bullets" and "I'm Not in Love," and the song's appeal continues. Three decades later, it would be reborn in one of the funniest-ever scenes in BBC Television's *The Mighty Boosh.* (YouTube "Boosh, I don't like cricket" for further enlightenment.)

"Pressure Drop"—Robert Palmer (1975)

How to choose? Between **the Clash**, **Keith Richards**, **the Specials**, and **Dubmood**, the world abounds with excellent versions of this song. But Robert Palmer did it first, a playful, almost calypso-flavored romp that titled his second solo album (following the sublime *Sneaking Sally Through the Alley*) and subverted the original's implicit warnings with a smooth New Orleans groove. The sadly missed Palmer is often best remembered for his 1980s output, and the music videos that once wallpapered MTV. But it is those first two albums that are the real lamb's bread.

"Soldering"—Hall and Oates (1975)

From John and Daryl's eponymous fourth album, this cover of Stanley Beckford and the Starlights' 1975 Jamaican hit was a peculiar thing to find wrapping up an album that otherwise delved deep into the blue-eyed-soul bag that the duo had made their own. But then you catch the irresistible chorus ("soldering" is a Jamaican euphemism for intercourse), and even the slickness is forgiven.

"Ain't It Strange"—The Patti Smith Group (1976)

Patti Smith was at the peak of her experimental powers when she and her eponymous band came to cut their second album together, *Radio Ethiopia*, in 1976; and "Ain't It Strange," a brooding dub cut deep in thrall to Rastafari's own fascination with Ethiopia, is the swirling mantric dynamite that ignites the remainder of the LP.

Neither was it a passing fancy. Smith and guitarist Lenny Kaye would sign the heavy-duty Jamaican toaster **Tappa Zukie** to their own Mer label; and when they played London in fall, 1976, Zukie was onstage alongside them, leading "Ain't It Strange" to even more abandoned heights.

A genuinely visionary artist, both as a toaster (which is how he initially became known) and a producer, Zukie was at his greatest in dub, but his most stirring across that run of mid-1970s singles that included "Pick Up the Rocker," "Marcus," "Tapper Roots," "Oh Lord," and, biggest of them all, "MPLA," widely regarded as being about the then-current Angolan Civil War (MPLA was the common acronym for the Popular Movement for the Liberation of Angola). But it was described by Zukie as concerning a far more international struggle. His MPLA represented the Members of the People's Liberation Army.

"Lucy in the Sky with Diamonds"—Elton John (1974)

Elton has spent his entire career veering between the sublime and the very, very silly. But a cat with no ears knows when he's just out there having fun, and this is one of those occasions. Inspired by the few weeks Elton spent at Dynamic Studios in 1973 (the sessions were transferred to France when it became apparent no work was getting done), this may not have been the first-ever attempt to reggaefy the Beatles. But as a U.S. chart-topper with composer John Lennon on pseudonymous guitar (Dr. Winston O'Boogie), it is certainly the first that people paid attention to, either howling in horror at Elton's sacrilege or applauding the verve with which he pulled it off.

"Sugartime"—Linda McCartney (1977)

Beatle Paul had already nodded in the direction of Jamaica when he chose to term the instrumental B-side of his "Give Ireland Back to the Irish" single a "version," from the Jamaican tradition of backing hit singles with their own backing track. Five years later, however, he and wife Linda were in Jamaica, recording at **Lee Perry**'s Black Ark studios, and it is true that you need to put your taste buds on a very long leash to actually *enjoy* this rendering of the old McGuire Sisters hit. But it is a lot of fun, and Perry kept it interesting, too. Go on, give it a go.

"D'yer Mak'er"—Led Zeppelin (1973)

Taken from their fifth album, "D'yer Mak'er" is worth infinitely more than the appalling pun with which it was titled; it is, in fact, the highlight of the entire *Houses of the Holy* album. It is also a merry little stroll that made an absolute mockery of Zeppelin's status as a heavy-metal band . . . but they'd never agreed with that, either. A lot of Zep fans describe "D'yer Mak'er" as an inconsequential little ditty, and probably squirmed even more when the superbly eccentric **Eek-A-Mouse** chose to cover it for a Jamaican hit single in 1991. But the old rocking warhorse rarely sounded like it was enjoying itself so much.

"Watching the Detectives"—Elvis Costello (1977)

Arguably **Elvis Costello**'s entire career has been an exercise in dilettantism, so it is no surprise to hear him heading dub-ward someplace or other. But at the outset of his career, with just one album of scratchy, angry protest punkers to his credit, and even his supporters muttering "Dylanesque" in his direction, "Watching the Detectives"' stygian bass lines and evil, echoed menace was an absolute revelation, both on vinyl and live. Especially the latter, where it was often expanded to both mammoth proportions and earthquake intentions.

"Midnight Rider"—Paul Davidson (1975)

The Allman Brothers are not a band you automatically look toward for hot slabs of reggae. But singer **Paul Davidson** took Gregg Allman's "Midnight Rider" and transformed it into one of *the* summertime smashes of 1975, all crashing offbeats and insistent sirens. And it was delightfully reborn three decades later when **Fatboy Slim** included it on his *Late Night Tales*

DJ mix collection alongside a clutch of more solid reggae hits, and a lot more besides.

"Meurglys III"—Van der Graaf Generator (1976)

Up there alongside King Crimson and Yes, VDGG (as it was short-handedly convenient to call them) were the ultimate seventies prog band. So what are they doing in here?

Well, right now they are jamming around a reggae riff that spun out of the band members' love of period Bob Marley albums. Organist Hugh Banton told the band's biographers Phil Smart and Jim Christopulos, "I'd really got[ten] into reggae, so sooner or later we were bound to do something like that." And although it's a comparatively short burst as the band drive toward the climax of the song, it's a rewarding one, all the same.

Emboldened, Clapton would return to reggae the following year for a supremely laid-back revision of the spiritual "Swing Low, Sweet Chariot" with an enthusiastic Dowd adding further encouragement by suggesting that they follow the Rolling Stones down to Dynamic Studios in Kingston to record both the single and Clapton's entire next album.

Comfortably ensconced within Kingston's Terra Nova hotel with his band, Clapton soon hooked up with one of Kingston's most enduring musicians, **Byron Lee**, to bring some authentic background flavor to the performance. Lee's group joined their bandmate on the resultant, contagiously impassioned bounce; and elsewhere, the studio seemed alive with ska/reggae legends.

Engineering the sessions was Graeme Goodall, whose Doctor Bird record label had been one of the key U.K. ska outlets during the early to mid-1960s. His assistant, **Carlton Lee**, was an accomplished producer in his own right; and another musical guest, **Peter Tosh**, needed no introduction whatsoever, being a member of the Wailers themselves. Regrettably, although the entire Wailers entourage stopped by the studio, Tosh was the only one who stepped up to a microphone; he would contribute guitar and vocals to two tracks on the sessions, his own "Burial" and "Whatcha Gonna Do."

Reggae was not to completely swamp Clapton's vision, of course; and once again we turn to bootlegs rather than the resultant album, *There's One in Every Crowd*, for enlightenment. But there would be a magnificent reggae reworking of **Bob Dylan**'s "Knockin' on Heaven's Door" released as a single later in 1975, and maybe Clapton's album had opened Dylan's own mind to the possibility of undertaking similar experiments.

By the early 1980s, the bard had recorded his own lightly reggaefied numbers "God Gave Names to All the Animals" (from the album *Slow Train Coming*) and "Dead Man, Dead Man" (from *Shot of Love*), and would soon be working with **Sly and Robbie**, the most legendary rhythm section in Jamaican musical history (albeit with very little reggae in sight—a typically Dylanesque joke).

In between those two moments, however, a lot of other great music had piled into earshot; and if Eric Clapton could not necessarily be described as its midwife, he was at least present at its birth. And we will get to that later in this book.

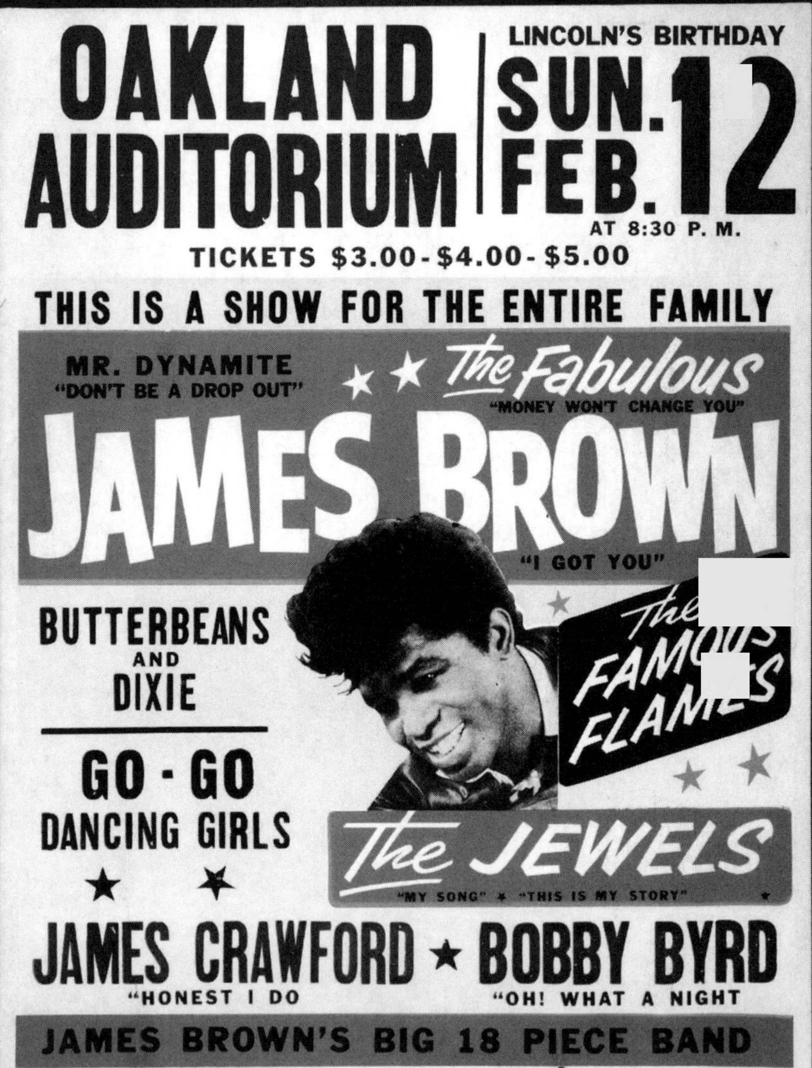

The billing says it all—the fabulous James Brown. (Author's collection)

2

NO NAME, NO NUMBER, NO LABEL: THE ROOTS OF REGGAE, AND OTHER STORIES

From Kingston to Coventry, from Orange County to Ocho Rios, and on to all points east and west, reggae music has encircled the world, and unleashed some of the biggest stars in modern music.

Bob Marley, **Dennis Brown**, **Gregory Isaacs**, Lee Perry, **John Holt**: the names are as legion as they are legendary, while Jamaica, the music's Caribbean island home, attracts as many music lovers as tourists these days, all hungry to visit the birthplace of the sounds they adore.

For despite its worldwide renown, reggae remains Jamaican music, and Jamaica's music. No matter that musical historians can trace its lineage back to any number of different musical forms, ranging from African drumming to American R&B, from British brass bands to Caribbean calypso. It was Jamaica that brought them all together in one humongous musical melting pot; and it is Jamaicans who have continued stirring that pot, throwing in new ingredients, and creating new hybrids to hurl onto the marketplace. From mento to dancehall, from ska to roots, from lovers rock to the darkest dub, reggae music has more faces than a crowded auditorium, but all are bound together beneath one triumphant banner.

The earliest records to preserve this remarkable creature emerged in the early 1960s as part of Jamaica's vibrant dance scene. For years, local DJs and record-store owners had been reliant on American music, booming out of massive and far-reaching transmitters on the Gulf Coast and beyond. Bebop, R&B, and swing all crossed the water to impact the Jamaican dance floors, recorded off-air onto reel-to-reel tape decks and then played back on the club scene; or, among the more adventurously inclined, picked up on vinyl from the U.S. itself. Businessmen and vacationers traveling to America would make a point of coming home with a bag stuffed with vinyl to be sold to local disc jockeys. Whose sharp ears, in turn, rapidly began isolating the kind of sounds that really got the audience going.

Today, our own ears might struggle to discover the lineage that connects, for example, the sounds of **Little Richard**, **Bo Diddley**, and **James Brown** to those that Jamaica would soon be producing, but it is there regardless.

Little Richard was a particular favorite on the dance floor. Just nineteen when he launched his recording career in 1951, the erstwhile Richard Wayne Penniman's earliest recordings were a jump blues–gospel hybrid that he learned from listening to Billy Wright records. Indeed, Wright was instrumental in Richard's first recording sessions, but the homage did not last for long. By 1953, Richard was moving hard into R&B, forming a touring band that scoured the American South, pounding out an increasingly raucous and (in the eyes of the era) outrageous blur of sound and vision.

Yet the Little Richard who leaps today out of old television and movie footage in a blur of black-and-white finery is but a pale specter of the brightly garbed, suggestively choreographed, and flamboyantly eccentric showman who touched down nightly in clubs across the region to belt out a solid set of high-octane freneticism, all delivered in a voice that could swing from a growl to a yowl within half a breath.

Signed to Specialty Records, and shifting his headquarters to New Orleans, by the end of 1955, Little Richard had already embarked upon the musical career that would help ferment rock 'n' roll for all posterity. "Tutti Frutti," "Long Tall Sally," "Slippin' and Slidin'," "Rip It Up," and "Ready Teddy" were all hits that same year; "The Girl Can't Help It" and "Lucille" were monsters in 1956; "Keep A Knockin'" and "Good Golly, Miss Molly" were

Top 10 goliaths in 1957–1958. And with every one, polite society recoiled a little bit further from the painted, screaming, gyrating madman who threatened to bring civilization crashing down around their ears with each new lyric.

It was the energy that Jamaica loved, the energy and the sheer defiance that Little Richard personified. Jamaica was still a British colony at the time, inching its way toward independence; but for now, it was firmly under the heel of a centuries-long allegiance to the crown and a rigid adherence to the "British way of doing things."

It was a mood that would grow increasingly rancorous as the so-called mother country lured more and more Jamaicans into immigrating to the U.K., only to discover that the British way of doing things was actually nothing like the fictions that tradition and colonial governors had perpetuated back on the island. Britain was gray, rainy, and depressing, and beset by both racism and snobbery. Even its youth was held down and back by so many rules and regulations that it was a wonder anybody ever smiled.

Certainly the likes of Little Richard were regarded among the most appalling aberrations the human race had ever hatched, and the rock 'n' roll music that was simultaneously making its way into British record stores was likewise being held up in the press, the TV, and even the halls of government as something that needed to be crushed at birth.

The Jamaican authorities were equally opposed. But Jamaica didn't care.

James Brown hit the airwaves. Another extravaganza, another musical maverick, Brown was as earthy as Little Richard was camp, but musically he could be just as outrageous, turning the taut rhythms and tight horns of R&B music into a clarion call of lust and hormones, a raging bull who saw red every place he looked.

New Brown singles were machine-gunned into the marketplace, and Jamaica snatched up the lot. There was little room for, or even awareness of, LP records in those days; the Jamaican music industry, such as it was, was oriented purely toward the short sharp shocks of the dance floor, hit single following hot 45, and so Brown peppered the island with one two-or-three-minute masterpiece after another. "Please, Please, Please," "Try Me," "I Want You So Bad," "I'll Go Crazy." Pick up any compilation of James Brown's 1950s singles, released on the fabulous old Federal label, and no less than Little Richard's output you will hear the sound of young Jamaica from 1955 to 1960. Brown's influence did not end there, either. By the early 1970s the Wailers were covering both "I Guess I'll Have to Cry, Cry, Cry," a Brown hit from 1964, and 1968's epochal "Say It Loud—I'm Black and I'm Proud."

But the major artists of the age offered up only a fraction of the music that kept Jamaica dancing. The key to a successful dance lay in having records that other, rival disc jockeys did not possess, and so the race ... or, more accurately, the war ... was on, the never-ending quest to build up the best collection of records and to keep it that way.

DJs would carefully tear the labels off new singles in their possession so that nobody could sneak a glance at what they were playing and grab a copy for themselves. Or they would deliberately mislead any spies in the audience by introducing one song as another, knowing that half a dozen DJs would be sending off for their own copy the very next day and would wind up with something utterly inappropriate instead—a ghastly MOR novelty song, for example, in place of a pounding R&B shrieker.

With New Orleans the first port of call for many Stateside-bound Jamaicans, and with that city's radio one of the defining presences on the island airwaves, the sounds of Louisiana's own unique R&B was inevitably at the forefront of Jamaica's musical consciousness.

Like every other teen of the era, the young Bob Marley, his own ambitions still in the process of being born, and visiting his own favorite dancehalls for his musical fix, was assailed nightly by the sounds of the Big Easy. He knew by heart the words (if not the titles and artists) of his favorite songs, and again we can share a slice of his upbringing by training our ears upon any of the great CD compilations of New Orleans's late-1950s output.

Professor Longhair was already a veteran of the French Quarter scene when he scored his first hit single, 1950's novelty-flavored

"Bald Head" (under the pseudonym Roy Byrd and His Blues Jumpers); and over the next five years his pounding piano-led R&B was as febrile as any, a livid tornado of rhythm and percussion over which the Professor's always-recognizable vocals first tangled, and then mangled, any sense of decorum that his band might have thought about introducing to the proceedings. Catch his contributions to the Bear Family label's *The New Orleans Sessions 1950 & 1953* CD, thirteen piano-pounding pinnacles that tear the laser from your CD machine and send it hurtling across the room.

Going simply by the strength of his vinyl, the Professor was comparable to both James Brown and Little Richard, long before anyone had heard either name. He might even have overtaken them, but a minor stroke put him out of action in the mid-1950s, and kept him there so long that his juke-joint madness had long since been eclipsed by the time he returned. By 1964, the Professor was working at a local record store, sweeping floors; when he did return to the industry, it would be too late.

Ultimately luckless, too, was **Lee Dorsey**, a performer who is best known to pop audiences for such novelty stompers as "Ya Ya" (which was subsequently covered by John Lennon), "Holy Cow," and "Working in the Coal Mine." Luckless, because he was also responsible for a lengthy string of truly ferocious R&B pounders cut for the Fury and Amy labels during the late 1950s and into the 1960s: "Ride Your Pony," "Get Out of My Life, Woman," "Go-Go Girl," "Yes We Can," and so on. All were Jamaican successes, and all play their part in the unfolding story. So do **Smiley Lewis**, **Fats Domino**, and **Dave Bartholomew**, names that just trip off the tongue like the musical mother's milk that they are. Bartholomew's "The Monkey" still possesses the capacity to astonish more than half a century after it was waxed, and so does the seething brew that is **the Spiders**' "Witchcraft."

Lurch lasciviously to Alma Lollypop, bruise your brains with Mr. Brown, wig out with Woo Woo Moore. The names mean little any longer, and the music they made is for the most part forgotten. But for anyone growing up in Trenchtown in the 1950s, it was the sound of savage freedom. If New Orleans was the geographical center of the Jamaican dancehalls' musical heartbeat, however, it was by no means the only source. Blues from Chicago, R&B from New York, and country from Nashville all fed into the sonic potpourri that was Jamaica—together, of course, with a helping hand from the island's own musical heritage, the sounds of mento.

An easy introduction. What calypso is to the neighboring islands of Trinidad and Tobago, mento is to Jamaica. It is local folk music, the sound of traditional songs played on the most rudimentary of instruments, and imbibed with the sheer joy of making a lot of noise and having a lot of fun. Pennywhistles and pots and pans, guitars and banjos, hand drums and thumb pianos, bamboo saxophones and homemade basses, mento was the sound of the Jamaican countryside, rural music that was largely looked down upon in the sophisticated cities, but was a part of most islanders' musical DNA regardless.

Like the folk music of any other nation, it didn't matter whether or not you actually liked the songs. You knew them, anyway, and you probably had your own words to them as well, for that is the defining nature of a true folksong. Constant evolution, constant change. It was only with the advent of recording technology at the start of the twentieth century that people started worrying about what the "definitive" lyric (or tune) might be for any given song. Prior to that, it was the message that mattered, not the words with which it was delivered, and a lot of the joy was sucked out of the medium once the ossification really set in.

The best mento in these pre-anal-retentive-archivist days were the songs that dealt with what we might call current affairs, usually presented in a humorous fashion and often imbibed with some bawdiness too. No less than today, political shenanigans were a popular topic, and where no concrete evidence of wrongdoing could be gathered, inventive slurs and allegations took their place. In the United States of the 1930s, underground bookstores did a roaring trade in so-called Tijuana Bibles, publishing appallingly licentious cartoons of current movie, radio, and political stars going about their quirky sexual business. A good mento performer was not above similar shenanigans.

Tunes were borrowed from wherever they could be found. Some were assuredly folk-flavored, adapted from melodies that were as old as the first Africans to arrive on the island as slaves. Others came from popular songs of the day; others still were simply tunes that everybody knew, from hymns to sea shanties to the National Anthem. So long as the lyrics made people smile, anything was permissible.

The first mento recordings date, as with most other Jamaican musical souvenirs, from the late 1950s. Arguably, this was actually the worst of times for mento, as the growing popularity of calypso on the international scene saw many Jamaican musicians leap aboard that bandwagon instead of their own jalopy. **Harry Belafonte** was a calypso superstar and, as Jamaica began opening up to tourism, it only followed that tourists would want to hear the music they associated with the Caribbean in general. In fact, there's a great joke in the 1978 movie ***Rockers***: local heroes **Inner Circle** pound through a solid roots-reggae number only for one of the watching tourists to turn around and ask, "This isn't calypso, is it?"

The same question had been asked twenty years before that, only now it was mento that fooled the foreigners. But it was preserved regardless. In the U.K., **Lord Power**'s now-legendary (and oft-revived) "Penny Reel" was a snigger-inducing success in 1957, and it captures all the wile and guile that made mento so irresistible. Provided you don't mind listening to songs about ladies who "shub" their "cushies."

Two mento albums to look out for: the British Decca label's marginally mistitled ***Authentic Jamaican Calypsos*** and Argo's ***Songs from Jamaica***, the latter of which was ironically performed by a Trinidadian, folklorist **Edric Connor**, but which was adamant via its liner notes that "[while] the calypso of Trinidad has ... become commercialized as a result of the development of the tourist industry ... this has not yet been the fate of the Jamaican songs."

Those same liners also indulged in a spot of crystal-ball gazing, and they were bang on the money. "Young, educated Jamaicans are beginning to turn to their own music; many of them know something of the old songs." Soon, **Prince Buster** would be recording two of the tunes that can be found on *Songs from Jamaica*, "Sammy Dead Oh" and "Day-Oh"; Max Romeo would cut a version of "Chi-Chi Bud Oh"; and there would be many more to come. Eric Morris recorded his own version of "Penny Reel"; **the Maytals** took "Naughty Little Flea" and re-created it as "Little Flea"; and **Phyllis Dillon** grasped an extraordinarily risqué mento titled "Don't Touch Me Tomato"—which, according to Bob Marley's mother, the future king of reggae could be heard delightedly singing in the late 1940s, by which time the song was already a golden oldie.

Mento was folk music, then. But blended with the rhythms of the R&B heat, it was soon to become a part of something else entirely.

Curtis Mayfield—singer-songwriter with attitude. (Photofest)

3

IMPRESSIONS OF CURTIS MAYFIELD: THE MAN WHO KEPT ON PUSHING

Of all the American artists whose music impressed itself upon the psyche of the young and, indeed, the older Bob Marley, few had the profound impact of **Curtis Mayfield and the Impressions**. Much of Marley and the Wailers' early music, across the dozens and dozens of sides they recorded for Coxsone Dodd's Studio One label, was visibly influenced by the Impressions, whose vocal harmonies and style was indeed a marvel to behold.

Neither was the traffic one-way. In 1964, Mayfield was commissioned to compile an album of what he considered to be the best sounds emanating from the island. He responded with the compilation ***The Real Jamaica Ska***, a twelve-track set that included cuts from Jimmy Cliff, **Winston Samuel**, **the Charmers**, **the Techniques**, and **Lord Creator**. Since reissued on CD (with two early Wailers cuts appended as bonus tracks), *The Real Jamaica Ska* is a tight little package whose reliance on vocal groups also demonstrates Mayfield's own appreciation of the island's debt to his music.

Mayfield is probably best remembered today for the solo career that he led in the decades following the Impressions' demise. In 1970, with the commercial tide in America turning toward the moods of such singer-songwriters as James Taylor, Cat Stevens, and Elton John, Mayfield released the album ***Curtis***, an avowedly political but also resolutely funky rock 'n' soul concoction that melted effortlessly into the new musical climate. "Move On Up" became a European hit single; Curtis talked of the influences of Chicago blues and Jimi Hendrix's guitar.

Bob Marley took note and, while few ears would ever compare his output of the next ten years with that of Mayfield's in stylistic terms, attitude and unconventionality would unite the two performers far more deeply than musical history records. Certainly Mayfield's ***Curtis/Live*** album was to electrify his following in exactly the same way as the Wailers' own *Live* disc, highlighting not the songs that made up the set list, but the sheer joy and electricity with which the artist approached the concert stage. Extending songs way beyond their studio confines, treating them as though they were new compositions and not hoary old favorites, Marley and Mayfield shared a live integrity that those two LPs in particular cement for all time.

Likewise, attempts to place Mayfield within the singer-songwriter bag were swiftly revealed to be as unambitious as those that described Marley as merely a reggae artist. His music, his vision and, most of all, his audience, far exceeded the confines of one single genre—a point that Mayfield's third solo album, the masterful *Roots*, might even have overstated with its broad sweeps of soul, R&B, funk, and rock all dramatically counterpointing the admitted sensitivity of his lyrics.

But it was with his next release, the ***Super Fly*** movie soundtrack, that Mayfield finally made the sociopolitical and musical transition that both his group and solo work had been aiming for, in exactly the way as *Exodus* would place Marley squarely on those same frontlines. That Mayfield's lyrics for the soundtrack amounted to an antidrug diatribe that sat in absolute opposition to the movie's own coke-fueled celebrations only amplified his achievement.

Super Fly (again like *Exodus*) was Mayfield's peak. His next LP, *Future Shock*, was a post-Vietnam concept album that took its lyrical message just a little too seriously, as though the writer had suddenly realized the weight of expectation that now hung over his head, and tried a bit too hard to justify it. It is still a great record, but it is also the sound of a performer struggling for the first time with a straitjacket of his own design.

One more album, ***Sweet Exorcist***, walked the thin line between polemics and politics, while a string of further movie soundtracks forgotten by almost everyone bar fans of the blaxploitation genre (and even by some of them) saw Mayfield meandering dangerously close to creative exhaustion. He later admitted that his slow drift down the commercial rankings was due in large part to simply trying to do too much at the same time, while his embrace of disco in the late 1970s effectively marked the end of Mayfield as a musical force.

He continued recording through the 1980s; and in 1989 a new soundtrack, hitting hard across the acclaimed movie *I'm Gonna Git You Sucka*, deservedly reawakened interest in his older work. The following year's ***Take It to the Streets***, too, revealed a major artist returning to the peak of his powers; and that same summer, Mayfield bestowed his blessings on the latest generation of streetwise R&B performers when he cut a sensational new single with rapper Ice-T, "Superfly 90."

But on August 13, onstage at an outdoor show at Wingate High School in Brooklyn, high winds blew over a lighting tower. It crashed onto the stage, onto Mayfield. Several of Mayfield's vertebrae were crushed and he was left quadriplegic, paralyzed from the waist down. His career came to a halt; and while there would be one last album, 1997's gospel-flavored ***New World Order***, his health continued to decline. He passed on December 26, 1999, at North Fulton Regional Hospital in Roswell, Georgia.

The obituaries that followed inevitably recalled Mayfield's political grandstanding; his frontline lyricism; and, of course, one of the sweetest soul voices of the era. But they also recalled something that his early to mid-1970s success often forgot: the decade he spent at the helm of the Impressions, without whom the entire face of black music might well have been altered; and without whom, Bob Marley would have sought out different musical heroes—and, perhaps, reached different musical conclusions.

Marley was not alone in his love of the Impressions. Dennis Brown's first-ever recording, at which the tiny preteen needed to stand on a box in order to reach the microphone, covered the Impressions' "No Man Is an Island." **Rupie Edwards** and **the**

Virtues cut a stunning version of their "Amen" in 1966; Byron Lee covered "Keep On Pushing" in 1967; and so on. The early Wailers themselves covered "Keep On Moving" in 1970, and titled their third album *Soul Rebel* from another Mayfield composition, while the *Exodus* album closes with a few impassioned moments from "People Get Ready." An astonishing compilation album could be drawn from all the Impressions covers that permeated the Jamaican dance floors of the 1960s; as astonishing in its own right as any good roundup of the band's own original greatest hits.

WAILERS GOT SOUL: TEN WAILING WAILERS COVERS

"African Herbsman"—Richie Havens (covered by the Wailers in 1971)

AKA "Indian Rope Man," in which form American singer Havens first recorded it on his *Richie P. Havens, 1983* album in 1969.

"And I Love Her"—The Beatles (1965)

The Beatles were as big in Jamaica as they were everyplace else!

"I Need You"—Chuck Jackson (1967)

A 1961 hit for American R&B star **Chuck Jackson**.

"Like a Rolling Stone"—Bob Dylan (1966)

Bunny and Bob share the vocals and the credit for rewriting Dylan's original 1965 lyric. But "time like a scorpion stings like warning" is a good enough line for Dylan himself to have penned.

"My Cup"—James Brown (1971)

Brown's "I Guess I'll Have to Cry, Cry, Cry," retitled from the lyric "my cup is running over."

"Say It Loud—I'm Black and I'm Proud" —James Brown (1969)

A keynote in the Wailers' "Black Progress" snatches a clearly recognizable slice of this Brown classic.

"Sugar Sugar"—The Archies (1970)

A 1969 chart-topper for a television cartoon, it was horrible in its original form and not seriously improved by the Wailers.

"Teenager in Love"—Dion (1965)

Dion's late '50s doo-wop classic showing off the Wailers' own remarkable harmonies.

"Ten Commandments of Love"—The Moonglows (1965)

Another reminder of the Wailers' doo-wop roots.

"This Train"—The Biddleville Quintette (1967)

A 1922 recording by the Florida Normal Industrial Institute Quartet is the earliest-known version of this traditional shouter, but most sources prefer to credit the 1927 Biddleville Quintette's version as the blueprint for the Wailers' cover. The Wailers also had a soft spot for the similarly hoary "Go Tell It on the Mountain."

Originally known as Jerry Butler and the Impressions in 1958, when "For Your Precious Love" gave them their first hit, it was with the departure of Butler at the end of the decade that the group truly hit its stride. Mayfield himself wrote Butler's biggest solo hit, 1960's "He Will Break Your Heart"; and, according to legend, he then plowed his earnings from that song into financing the Impressions' relocation to New York, where they recorded the demo that caught the ear of the ABC-Paramount label.

In 1961, "Gypsy Woman" became the Impressions' first major hit; "It's Alright" followed, and then came "Keep On Pushing," a civil-rights anthem that melded perfectly with the spirit of the times, In terms of voices raised to sing along, it aligned the Impressions alongside the folkier delights of Dylan and Joan Baez in the vocabulary of marchers and demonstrators. Again, the parallels with Marley and the Wailers' career in Jamaica are unmistakable, as they too utilized the deceptive sweetness of their vocal sound to mask the often-gritty sociopolitical content of their lyrics. And were rewarded for the subterfuge with an audience that hung on their every word.

"I'm So Proud" and 1965's emotion-soaked "People Get Ready" were equally hard-hitting and, in many ways, equally deceptive. Today, those songs are so entrenched in our nation's musical/political lexicon that it seems hard to believe there was ever a time when people were unaware of the true nature of their content. (Covered by Bob Marley on *Exodus*, years later, "People Get Ready" was among four Impressions songs included in Spike Lee's Million Man March–themed film *Get On the Bus*.)

Yet that was the case. To adherents of the civil-rights movement, the Impressions' message was obvious. But to the average folk around town who treated music as nothing more than something to listen to while they were driving, the songs were just sweet soul sing-alongs. It would be 1968, when a string of U.S. radio stations banned the group's MLK-inspired "We're a Winner," before the Impressions' so-joyous subversion was finally exposed.

The Impressions retaliated by discarding the smart suits and ties that had hitherto been their chosen stage wear, and turning up instead in the street clothes that themselves were a badge of recognition in the civil-rights movement—wide pants, turtleneck sweaters, leather jackets, and sailor's caps. It was the image of revolution, yet the group did not preach insurgence. Rather, they advocated moderation and common sense, asking, "How long have you hated your white teacher?" in 1969's "Choice of Colors," then reiterating their dismissal of race war on its B-side, the still-potent "Mighty Mighty (Spade and Whitey)" (a song that Mayfield was still opening his live show with years later).

The Impressions had reached their peak; Mayfield's growing conviction that he was destined for a solo career would soon see him step outside of the band. He attempted to keep both projects alive for a short time, but by 1971 he had departed. That same year, the unknown-outside-of-Jamaica group that most consciously echoed the Impressions' own convictions, musically and politically, arrived in London to sign their first-ever international record deal.

For believers in fate, and nature's hatred of vacuums, it was as if the universe itself had spoken aloud. The King is dead. Long live the King.

After all that, deciding where to start a Curtis Mayfield collection should be a no-brainer, with his first three solo albums and a decent Impressions collection generally regarded as the neon-lit portals to a universe of magical experience. But just as many Bob Marley fans earned their introductions to the Wailers via the more contemporary-sounding remixes that started emerging during the 1990s, so Mayfield too has not escaped the attentions of those who would modernize the miraculous. And, like Marley, he came out smiling at the end of the process.

We have grown so sadly accustomed over the years to hearing one bad remix collection after another that it often comes as a surprise when one actually worth listening to appears. And even more of a surprise when the artist under the remixing hammer is Curtis Mayfield. His catalogue, after all, rates among the most peerless of them all, with sounds and production values that simply refuse to date, no matter how fast time passes these days.

How unappetizing, then, is the prospect of spending close to seven minutes listening to Grandmaster Flash shout "adrenaline" over "We're a Winner"? Especially when he accompanies himself with those quaint scratchy-record sounds that, contrarily, have dated *horribly* since they were first developed in the early 1980s. What possible improvements could King Britt bring to "Little Child Runnin' Wild" that Mayfield himself omitted the first time around? And what, precisely, do *you* think a Blaze Roots DJ mix of "Freddie's Dead" might sound like?

Check expectations at the door. ***Mayfield Remixed: The Curtis Mayfield Collection*** is a joy from start to (almost) finish ... yes, the Grandmaster Flash stab is a little overbearing, while "Do Do Wap Is Strong in Here" wasn't one of Mayfield's most drop-dead gorgeous classics to begin with. But balance those comparative failures with the absolute triumphs that stack up elsewhere—from Louie Vega's opening "Superfly" through a stunning "vocal mix" of "Move On Up" and onto a closing salvo of "People Get Ready" and "Pusherman"—and even the sometimes self-consciously *modern* meddling of the re-mixers can only catapult the best of Mayfield even further into your consciousness.

Perhaps, if you're hyper-holy about your Mayfield, *Remixed* may leave you cold and uncaring. But if they'd invented twelve-inch remixes when he was in his prime, at least half of this material would already be in your collection. And the rest deserves to join it there.

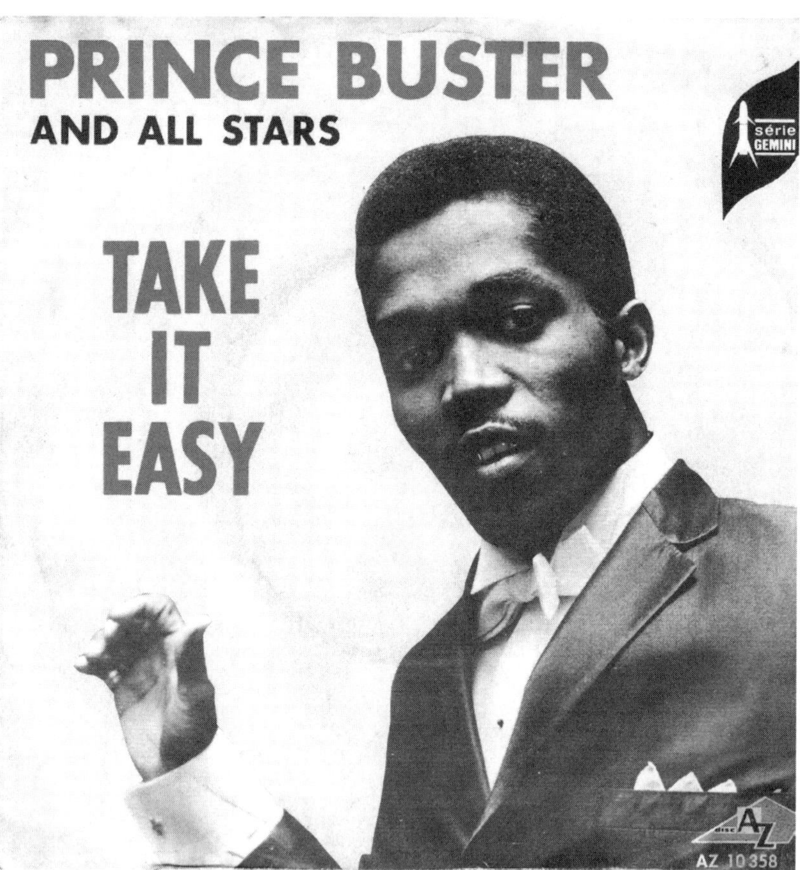

Prince Buster, the King of Ska. (Author's collection)

4

MAKE WAY FOR THE PRINCE: THE TEN COMMANDMENTS OF BUSTER

The story of reggae is the story of dance, because that, essentially, is what reggae is: a catchall title for the succession of dances that for the past near-sixty years have swept first Jamaica, then the Caribbean, and ultimately the world.

Ska and rocksteady were both popular dances during the early 1960s. Dub, toasting, lovers rock, roots, and slacker do refer to distinct musical styles, but dancehall was so named because that's where the music was at its most popular: in the dancehalls. Even reggae itself started life as a dance before its name was seized upon by Western fans in the late 1960s to become a way of life. Prior to that, most British and Americans knew Jamaica's music as "bluebeat," from the name of one of the most successful U.K. record labels. And in Jamaica itself, it was simply music, the music that arose from the sound systems, the traveling DJ setups that were the heart and soul of what passed for the local music industry.

At the same time as one pack of entrepreneurs were still soaking the labels off their import 45s and lively-ing up the dancehalls with hot American R&B, so were others taking the first strides toward creating an even more unique hybrid. In tiny studios across the island, the first pioneering producers were adapting popular songs with local musicians, rewriting and rewiring certain lyrics and riffs, and then underpinning them with a taste of Jamaica's own musical heritage, the syncopated rhythms that would eventually come to define the country's entire recording industry.

It was a popular approach; so popular that, by the end of the

1950s, those battered and label-less American imports were all but forgotten, as would-be record producers began emerging from every corner, scraping together the money to buy, or hire, a few rudimentary pieces of recording equipment; gathering together a coterie of reliable musicians who would become the studio's house band; and then combing Jamaica's talent shows and club scene in search of potential singers.

Many of Jamaica's earliest record producers were running their own sound systems as well. Names like Prince Buster, Coxsone Dodd, **Duke Reid**, and Leslie Kong rose up, the creators of exciting 45s that were recorded in hours and pressed just as quickly, then raced from the studio to the dancehalls to be aired to the masses that very same evening. And between them, this quartet would be responsible for launching the age of ska, a period of roughly five years at the start of the 1960s during which almost every record released in Jamaica was set to the same madly compulsive beat—the ska.

There was no shortage of performers: bands like the Wailers, **the Blues Busters**, the Techniques, and Toots and the Maytals; singers like **Derrick Morgan**, **Desmond Dekker**, **Freddie McGregor**, and Jimmy Cliff; duos like **Stranger and Ken**, **Derrick and Patsy**, and **Keith and Enid**; and, of course, the legendary **Skatalites**, the greatest bunch of session men in the world.

Overnight, it seemed, all of these and so many more rose to brilliant prominence. A young man might walk into a studio and declare himself a singer. The producer would ask him to prove it, and set the tapes rolling immediately. Then, if it was good enough, it would be playing at the dancehall within a day or two of the recording. If the record did well, the singer would be invited back; if it didn't, he'd just walk a few blocks and drop by the next studio, and the whole process would begin again.

Many careers that began during the very infancy of the Kingston recording scene would still be going strong decades later, constantly shifting and adapting their style to suit whichever music the dancehalls demanded next. Others would fall by the wayside, but are remembered regardless, the creators of some of the most exhilarating records ever made, all of them set to the pounding, honking, and irresistibly contagious ska beat.

There were no record contracts in those days. There were no major labels, none of the businesslike machinery with which we associate the modern music industry. Recording arrangements were made on a handshake; records were cut on a budget; and it was not at all unusual for one singer to bring out a dozen singles in a year, every one for a different producer and each therefore on a different label.

It was that freedom that allowed reggae music to develop as fast as it did. Through the 1960s, singers and musicians alike were constantly striving to introduce new musical elements into the sound, something that nobody else had ever thought of.

Some looked toward *grounations*, Rastafarian religious ceremonics, and borrowed the insistent tribal drums as a backdrop to their music. Others sped up the beat or, contrarily, slowed it way down. Some stripped away the vocals and guitars, and allowed the bass and drums alone to do the legwork, then layered weird sounds and sound effects over the ensuing rhythm. The first time anyone heard **Augustus Pablo**, for example, he was playing a melodica, an instrument most westerners hadn't heard since music class at school! By the time Jamaica took its independence from Britain, the island seethed to a sound that had scarcely been imaginable a few years earlier. And seated at the top of the pile was one man whose music remains the template for all that was to emerge throughout that first decade of musical freedom.

Prince Buster is the (almost) undisputed crown prince of 1960s Jamaica; he is a name that everybody knows, pounding out a unique sound that everyone can identify. And not only in Jamaica.

Buster's influence haunts every great record of the British-ska sixties as they blended the rude-boy skank with the skinhead moonstomp, and it fired every worthwhile moment spawned by the Specials- and **Madness**-led 2-Tone era. Buster's imagery permeated that incredible upsurge in ska awareness that hallmarked the American 1990s; and almost fifty years on from what even he would call his musical peak, he's still out there. He calls himself Prince, but really, he's a force of nature.

Former boxer Cecil Bustamente Campbell, "Buster" to everyone who knew him, was one of Coxsone Dodd's crowd, DJ-ing the mid-1950s Jamaican sound-system circuit. But whereas other Jamaican musicians and DJs remained content working with (and cutting records that aped) existing American sounds, Buster dreamed of designing a new musical soundscape. Something that he called "a Jamaican sound." That was why he christened his own sound system the Voice of the People, and started performing his own compositions: he wanted to send the tyranny of the American beat back to the land that spawned it, replacing it with something unique. Jamaican music, sung in Jamaican style, delivered in the Jamaican dialect. Set to a sound that had never been heard before.

He took his inspiration from childhood—his and many other people's. The British occupation had been at its colonial peak when Buster was a boy; and every day it seemed that the soldiers would parade through the streets, marching to the stirring sounds of the military drum. With jazz drummer Drumbago Parkes aping that primal sound, and guitarist Jah Jerry and tenor saxman Stanley "Ribs" Notice storming over the top, Buster knew from the beginning that he was on to a winner. Little boys, he said, would always follow the march.

Simplistic, even rural, Buster's earliest efforts were despised by his rivals. They were not music, they were kid's stuff; they were not proficient, they were amateur. In the same way that the punks of 1977 became outcasts in the eyes of the progressive-rock cognoscenti, Buster and his records were seen as clattering throwbacks that had no musical merit whatsoever. On one occasion, preparing for a session at the Jamaica Broadcasting Company studios, Buster's efforts were almost laughed out of the room by the serious jazz and R&B players who hung around to watch.

But Buster had the last laugh. That may have been the day that he cut no less than thirteen songs in a single session, and every one of them became a hit. They included future classics like

Bunny and Skitter's "Chubby" and future game-changers like the **Folkes Brothers**' "Oh Carolina," a record that combined mento lightness with *nyahbinghi* freedom, matched to the rhythm of that marching army and emerging a subversive underground hit that other producers, Buster later swore, were trying to copy the moment they heard it. Or the moment they saw how well it went down at Buster's next dance.

Buster courted controversy. A dispute with Derrick Morgan, a singer and producer with whom he worked early in the 1960s, transferred from a war of words to a war in music, with both artists releasing new singles that told their side of the argument in brutal fighting tones. Soon, the conflict was so intense that the two performers' own fans were clashing in the nightclubs and threatening to provoke even greater violence. Finally, the Jamaican government itself stepped in, organizing a truce between the two singers, followed by a highly publicized reconciliation. None of which damaged the superstars' popularity in the slightest.

Buster was tireless, cutting his own singles in one breath, producing others in the next. The litany of new bands unearthed by Buster is almost endless, but it is certainly topped by the legendary Toots and the Maytals. And the sequence of singles that pumped out of the Buster factory throughout the early 1960s included some of the greatest records Jamaica had ever heard. "Blackhead Chineman" and "Thirty Pieces of Silver," immortalizing the Morgan contretemps. "Time Longer Than Rope," "Independence Song," "My Sound That Goes Around," "One Hand Wash the Other," "Cowboy Comes to Town," "Fake King," "They Got to Go," and "These Are the Times." Every one was a slice of killer contagion; every one left his audience ravenous for more.

Buster's first stone-cold classic was 1963's "The Ten Commandments of Man," a code of dress, behavior, and morality aimed at his womenfolk that traveled from "One! Thou shall have no other man but me!" through to "Ten! Thou shall not covet thy neighbor's dress... for I will not give thee anything but what you actually need for your purpose." A record like that would probably be incinerated by righteous wrath before it ever reached the streets today.

Further treasures followed. "Madness" gave its name, sixteen years later, to the 2-Tone band of the same name; "Sodom and Gomorrah" was an incisive condemnation of the persecution faced by Jamaica's Rastafarians. Every one of them sounds as dynamic today as it did at the time.

In 1964, to the utter mystification of watching tourists and sightseers, Buster represented Jamaica at the New York World's Fair; that same year he played his first British shows, guesting on television's legendary *Ready Steady Go!*, where he was blown away by his reception. He hit the local club circuit, and the cheers drowned out the PA. He recorded a new single, the tremendous "Wash Wash," with local organ hero Georgie Fame, and wrote another new song, "Ghost Dance," reflecting upon the pangs of homesickness that occasionally assailed him while he was away.

Buster's biggest ever hit, "Al Capone," followed, all pulsating rhythms and screeching car brakes, chattering machine guns and insistent vocals. "Don't call me scarface! My name is Capone. C-A-P-O-N-E. Capone." A U.K. Top 20 hit in early 1967, and still his best-known record, "Al Capone" was the record that broke ska into the British mainstream in the same way as "Oh Carolina" had been the record that introduced it to Jamaica. But again, Buster did not rest on his laurels. Instead, he introduced the island to his next creation, the righteous judiciary of Judge Dread.

Outlaw "rude boy" society was now one of the staple themes of Jamaican music, the subject of records as disparate as Buster's "Johnny Cool"; Desmond Dekker's "007 (Shanty Town)" (named for a youth camp and not, as is often claimed, for James Bond); and, best of all, Derrick Morgan's "Rougher Than Rough (Rudies in Court)."

The song was widely regarded as the ultimate celebration of rude-boy insolence. Called before the magistrate to answer a battery of typical rude-boy charges—looting, shooting, and, oddly, mooning, the rude boys sat through the Judge's opening remarks, and then responded in chorus. "Your honor ... *rudies don't fear!*"

What a statement that was, the ultimate roar of youthful defiance, a kick in the teeth for every last stale convention of justice and authority. The record was a massive hit, and Jamaica's rude boys reveled in the perceived invincibility that the song conveyed upon them. But not for long. For here came Buster's "Judge Dread," rising in court to address the sniggering, posturing brats and declaring, "I am the rude boy now … and *I don't care!*" He then handed out the longest prison sentences he could think of; and when a little voice rose out of the hubbub and pleaded meekly for clemency, Judge Dread did not even need to consider his response. He handed down an extra hundred years of imprisonment. And while the Judge raved and raged, the defeated barristers sadly chorused, "You're rough, you're tough …"

The song was a sensation, and it didn't matter that it was only a song. The rude boys' invincibility had been publicly punctured, and not even by the determinations of society itself. By one of their own idols!

THE OTHER JUDGE DREAD

Born Alex Hughes, but forever remembered as **Judge Dread**, Buster's greatest creation lived on in a white Londoner namesake who had followed Jamaican music for years, and who began cutting his own reggae records to play when he DJ-ed at various clubs around the city. His specialty was the super-spicy, borderline-obscene double entendre, which he lewdly recited to the instrumental "versions" that appeared on the B-sides of so many Jamaican 45s. It was only inevitable that he would soon be making his own records. What was more shocking was how successful they became.

In 1972, Judge Dread's wryly titled successor to Buster's "Big 5," "Big Six," brought him an entirely unexpected hit record; over the next five or six years, Dread was seldom away from the British charts. This despite the vast majority of his records being so rude (in a juvenile, nursery-rhyme kind of way) that they couldn't even be played on the radio!

"Big Six" was followed by a host of even greater-dimensional skankers: "Big Seven," "Big Eight," "Big Nine," and, of course, "Big One." But while his critics (of whom there were, and still are, many) insist that Dread did little more than rehash the kind of ribald verses that had been circulating Britain's schoolyards for decades, Dread and his supporters were having the time of their lives: "Mary had a little sheep, she could not stop it grunting; she took it down the garden path and kicked . . ." *Et cetera*.

Nothing was sacred. The Judge showed a genuine grasp of pointless bathroom humor: "Two old ladies sitting in the bath; one blew off and the other one laughed...'Oh, look, bubbles!'" remains a belly laugh however many times you hear it. He took **Serge Gainsbourg**'s erotic classic "Je T'Aime, Moi Non Plus" and transformed it into a figure of fun. He immortalized life on the farm by celebrating "Up with the Cock."

He mocked transvestites, and he reveled in middle-aged skinhead thuggery. He even released one single, "Molly," that did not have the merest ghost of rudeness hanging around it, and still found himself banned by the BBC. His very name was sufficient to strike judgmental Dread into the corridors of broadcasting power. Ten Top 50 hits in under five years is a fabulous achievement under any circumstances. Ten Top 50 hits without an iota of radio or television support is little short of miraculous, while a succession of albums, ***Dreadmania*** and ***Working Class 'Ero*** included, were similarly successful.

Where Judge Dread's significance truly lies, however, is in a fact that makes lot of reggae fans (especially in the U.K.) so uncomfortable that they will howl abuse at its very mention. In U.K. chart terms, he was not simply the most successful homegrown reggae artist of all time. For many years, he was the most successful reggae artist full-stop; and while serious music fans continue to decry his often childish humor, dismissing him as a one-trick pony when compared to the giants of Jamaican lewdness (Lee Perry, Prince Buster, Max Romeo), the fact that he kept the trick going for over five years of hits itself became a feat to celebrate. Indeed, even after the hit machine finally ran out of steam, Judge Dread continued recording, continued performing, and presumably continued growing. By the time of his death in March 1998, he was reported to have reached "Big 15."

One can only wonder where he kept it.

Immediately, other artists came to the convicted rude boys' defense. A plaintive Lee Perry begged for Judge Dread to "Set Them Free"; **Honeyboy Martin** tried to outmaneuver the Judge with the menacing **"Dreader Than Dread."** And Buster, who by now was bemused by the whole thing, announced that he would sort everything out with his next single, "The Barrister (The Appeal)," the story of the rude boys' appeal.

For weeks, Jamaica waited. It has been said that even among real-life legal verdicts, few had been so eagerly awaited as this one. Nobody doubted that the rude boys would be freed; in fact, as the record's release date drew nearer, freedom parties were announced for dancehalls across the island.

The optimism was contagious. It was also misplaced. Judge Dread didn't care what the public thought; he didn't give a hoot about popular opinion. He jailed the barrister, then warned the plaintiffs that if they came back to his court again, "I will lynch you." Six thousand years.

There would be a happy ending. Probably tiring of the entire surreal affair, Buster finally allowed Judge Dread a change of heart in one final single, recalling the jailed quartet back to court, then producing horn player Rico Rodriguez and dancing the accused to freedom. "Judge Dread Dance (The Pardon)" became the biggest hit in the entire cycle.

Buster's career did not end there, of course. He continued turning out some great records, helping to initiate Jamaica's late-1960s fascination with sexually explicit lyrics via such delights as "Wreck a Pum Pum" (to the tune of "Little Drummer Boy"!), "Pussy Cat Bite Me," and "Big 5." He moved smoothly, too, into the rocker rebel scene of the early 1970s, still recording but with less regularity. The effervescent "Dance Cleopatra Dance" proved he was still a power when he wanted to be; but more and more he settled into the role of a backseat driver, content to leave the new music to the newer artists. He was content, too, to relax in his status as godfather to an entire new generation.

By the time of the 2-Tone explosion of the late 1970s, Buster was already a figure of legend, to be invoked in tribute, cover, and loyal imitation. The screeching brakes that launch the Specials' "Gangsters" debut single were lifted from "Al Capone"; Madness recorded his "One Step Beyond" and honored him with "The Prince." Two decades after that, Buster was back on the U.K. chart with a remake of the old hit "Whine and Grine"; and today, deep into his seventies and residing in Miami, he still occasionally gets up to perform. And he remains magnificent.

Trojan Records presents the best of Toots and the Maytals. (Author's collection)

5

54-46 WAS THEIR NUMBER: TOOTS AND THE MAYTALS

More than the Wailers, more than Prince Buster, more than Jimmy Cliff, the story of the Maytals is the story of Jamaican music. From the outset of their career in 1962, through the stylistic convolutions of the next two decades and onto frontman **Toots Hibbert**'s pursuits since the band's demise, the Maytals charted and occasionally even instigated every significant sea change of the 1960s and 1970s. They were the archetypal ska band when that was *de rigueur*; they helped birth rocksteady when the tempos slowed to menacing rhythms; and it was the they who introduced the word "reggae" to the musical lexicon in 1968. Their ***Reggae Got Soul*** album, in 1976, confirmed Jamaican music's heritage in the world of American R&B, and Bob Marley called them the single greatest influence on the Wailers' own career.

A vocal trio comprising Toots Hibbert, Jerry Matthias, and Raleigh Gordon, the Maytals came together in the early 1960s under the aegis of producer Coxsone Dodd. It was he who cut their first single, "Hallelujah," but it was Hibbert who made the vinyl seethe. A singer firmly cut in the James Brown mold, he was alternately abandoned and evangelical, explosive and corrosive, spiritual and spirited, fueled by a dynamism that sent a sonic boom resonating across all that the Maytals set their sights on: "Fever," "Six and Seven Books of Moses," "Marching On"; the spirituals "He Will Provide" and "Shining Light"; "I'll Never Grow Old," "Study War No More" (AKA "Down by the Riverside"), "Matthew Mark," and "Helping Ages Past." The band even cut an album,

1964's ***Presenting the Maytals***, in an age when LPs were an extravagance that few other stars could even dream of.

The group could handle anything. Dodd was big on ballads, and many of the Maytals' early sides highlighted this side of their brilliance. But after they broke with him and went to work with Prince Buster in 1964, it was their drop-dead dangerous side that the producer wanted to focus on. The sequence of singles that devoured "Dog War," "Bet You Lied," "He's Real," "Goodbye Jane," "My Old Flame," "You Got Me Spinning," "Pain in My Belly," and "Domino" represents one of the most fluid conflagrations in ska history, not only maintaining the band's commercial star, but pushing them to the forefront of rude-boy culture, too.

The rudies were the guiding force behind the music's next stylistic convolution, and the Maytals moved with it. It was spring 1965, and the kids no longer wanted to "do the ska." The rocksteady was taking over the dance floors, slower and more considered, cool music for cool rudies. The pumping horns and skipping rhythms of old were set aside. The bass now drove the song, and the very pulse of the music was fundamentally altered.

Some of the greatest records of the age were those that spoke directly to the rudies. Some strove to downplay the cult's violent temperament at a time when the headlines were filled with rudie outrage: the Maytals' "Bam Bam," winner of Jamaica's first-ever Independence Song Festival; **Dandy Livingstone**'s "A Message to You, Rudie"; **the Rulers**' "Don't Be a Rude Boy"; and Derrick Morgan's "Cool the Rudies" all called for the new cult to remain calm and not look for trouble.

But the Wailers' "Rude Boy" and "Jailhouse," Desmond Dekker's "007 (Shanty Town)," Peter Tosh's "I Am the Toughest," and a string of Prince Buster 45s looked at the other side of the coin, to make folk heroes out of the street fighters, and street fighters out of the musicians. The Maytals' own standing was only amplified then, in 1966, when Hibbert was found guilty of possessing marijuana and sentenced to eighteen months' imprisonment. It would be 1968 before the group resurfaced. But they made up for lost time with two of the most memorable hits of the age.

THE DIRTY DOZEN

Shortly before the end of erotic author Chrissie Bentley's 2012 novella *Jamaica: What I Did on My Summer Vacation 2*, the story's heroine finds herself onstage with an unnamed reggae superstar, a man who scored eight #1's a decade before but now sings for fun around the hotels and dancehalls of the Jamaican coast.

He has two very separate acts. The one that he gears toward the tourists wraps up his own greatest hits, and those of various others—he seduces the novel's heroine by offering her a private concert of old Bob Marley songs. The other, which is tailored for the hardcore dancehall crowd, is somewhat raunchier, and it climaxes with the singer himself climaxing, at the conclusion of a live sex performance that he accompanies with a lyric that, even by the no-holds-barred standards of modern erotica, leaves nothing to the imagination.

Where erotica scarcely goes, however, reggae has been dancing for decades. As far back as 1969, Max Romeo aroused the ire of the BBC when his "Wet Dream" became an absolutely unwelcome British hit, with its explicit insistence and raunchy rapport. And we've already seen what Judge Dread got up to. Even before that, however, Jamaican dancehalls had echoed, and chuckled, to the sounds of explicit sexuality, and they continue to do so today. The following twelve songs, dating from the 1960s and early 1970s, should therefore be investigated by consenting adults only. Because this is X-rated reggae music.

"Don't Touch Me Tomato"—Phyllis Dillon (1967)

Beloved of the junior Bob Marley, the delectable Ms. Dillon invites her lover to touch her here, touch her there . . . but please stay away from her salad bowl.

"Dub a Dawta"—Big Joe and Fay (1973)

An aspiring singer accidentally turns up in a bordello instead of the studio, and it is difficult to adequately describe what happens next as Fay moans and groans over clattering percussion, and Big Joe answers her occasional comments in a defensive tone (but, presumably, with a very satisfactory performance).

"How Your Pantie Get Wet?"—Stranger and Gladdy (1971)
Well, it wasn't raining, it wasn't too sweaty, and she didn't go swimming, so all our heroes want to know is, "How your pantie get wet?" And they don't seem to believe their lady's response.

"Hole Under Crutches"—Max Romeo and Fay (1970)
The ever-simmering Fay again, revising the old "There's a Hole in My Bucket" with a surprisingly underdeveloped Max Romeo. "Have you put it in already? How come I can't feel anything?"

"Papa Do It Sweet"—Lloyd and Patsy (1972)
Two lovers reunite after an absence, it seems. And they get reacquainted ...

"Ram You Hard"—The Bleechers (1969)
His girl told him outright that he wasn't much of a man. His response has very little to do with sheep.

"Wreck a Buddy"—The Soul Sisters (1969)
A female riposte to Prince Buster's "Wreck a Pum Pum," misappropriating "Little Drummer Boy" once again in this lament for a ticklish pum pum. Buster cut an entire album of songs in this vein, named for his own starting point and, needless to say, it is magnificent.

"Cock Stiff and Hard"—George Anthony (1968)
Leaves so little to the imagination that...plus, it is possibly the only song in which a "pum pum" is described as being "deep...a reservoir."

"Play with Your Pussy"—Max Romeo (1973)
Max sings the virtues of his lover's little fat cat. And don't miss the name-check of Judge Dread ("You know, that rude guy") over the intro.

"I Want a Grine"—Glen Adams & the Hippy Boys (1970)

"Tonight's the night, I want, I want a grine." There are no mixed meanings here!

"Birth Control"—Lloydie and the Lowbites (1970)

Feline hygiene would appear to be on Lloydie's mind, as he dispatches Doris to wash the pussy. It's dirty, apparently.

"Scorpion"—Nora Dean (1975)

Reprising her biggest hit from five years previous, Ms. Dean has removed the barbed wire from her lover's underpants, and replaced it with a scorpion. Oh, mamaaaaa!

The first was the pounding frenzy of "54-46, That's My Number," titled from the singer's prison number, and taking its theme from Hibbert's belief that he (and many others like him) was jailed not for his "crime," but for his religion—he was a strict Rastafarian.

The second was "Do the Reggay" and, with this pair announcing their return in the most uncertain terms, the Maytals launched into a period of absolute invincibility. "One Eyed Enos," "Schooldays," "Don't Trouble Trouble," "Scare Him," "Struggle," and "We Shall Overcome" each reiterated the group's street-tough reputation. The anthemic "Monkey Man" dented the U.K. Top 50 in 1970. "Pressure Drop" went on to earn covers from Robert Palmer, the Clash, and Keith Richards. The Maytals were integral to the soundtrack of the movie ***The Harder They Come***; and in 1973 the newly renamed Toots and the Maytals cut the seminal ***Funky Kingston*** with producer Chris Blackwell, the head of the Island Records label.

The Maytals joined the Wailers on Island Records in 1975, and the following year's *Reggae Got Soul* became one of the most talked-about (and deservedly so) albums of the year, raising the group's profile so high that even a lengthy return to Jamaica, cutting largely religious-themed 45s for the local audience alone, could not damage their international renown. Three years elapsed before the Maytals released 1979's ***Pass the Pipe***; but when the band returned to the U.K. to tour, their Hammersmith Palais show not only sold out in record time, it also got the group into the *Guinness Book of World Records* for what was then the fastest live album ever released. ***Toots Live*** was mastered, pressed, packaged, and in the stores within a day of the final encore.

Toots and the Maytals' final album, ***Knockout***, was released in 1981; the trio broke up soon after, bowing out with a revival of 1966's "Bam Bam" that proved to be a highlight of the soundtrack to the *Countryman* movie, and with a riotous slot at the 1982 Reggae Sunsplash. Hibbert then launched a solo career, occasionally broadening his musical horizons far beyond reggae, even earning a Grammy nomination for 1988's ***Toots in Memphis***, his personal take on the classic Stax material that he and the Maytals had so effortlessly been rivaling back in the mid-1960s.

Today, Hibbert tours again with a reborn Maytals; he records occasionally and enjoys his legend. One that is spread over a wealth of albums, a goldmine of compilations, and, of course, a few stellar live albums. Listen, and you will see exactly what Bob Marley was talking about.

Lee "Scratch" Perry live at the Rocktambule Festival in Grenoble, France, 2009.
(Wikimedia Commons/Saruman)

6

A MAN CALLED SCRATCH: THE BLACK ARK OF LEE PERRY

By the end of the 1960s, the scratchy syncopation of the earliest Jamaican records had long since given way to a more powerful, mood-enhanced sound in an explosion that brought many of reggae's most powerful names to the fore; it also saw some of the older heroes looking decidedly downcast.

Bob Marley and the Wailers, for example, had been recording since 1962, and enjoyed a sizable run of local hits during the first half of the decade. Now, however, they were somewhat less vibrant, supplanted at the top of the chart by acts like **the Heptones**, John Holt's **Paragons**, the recently revived Maytals, and many more.

But then the Wailers linked with producer Lee Perry—one of the maverick geniuses who had so shaken the local music scene over the past few years—and suddenly the band launched into a period of renewed success and brilliance, singing defiant lyrics spread over compulsive rhythms, all of it set to propel reggae into its next major mood change: the roots-reggae sound that confirmed the music's outlaw status.

Like the protest songs of early-1960s America, or the punk rock of late-1970s Britain, roots music was rebel music, the sound of a generation rising up against the iniquities inherent in the political and social system of the day, and demanding change. Sometimes they received it, too. Jamaican elections throughout the 1970s were accompanied every step of the way by the sound of reggae, praising or decrying the candidates, suggesting reforms and promises, condemning lies and misinformation.

Dillinger, **Junior Murvin**, **Culture**, **the Wailing Souls**, and so many more burst into prominence; many of the roots movement's greatest stars were DJs who took to "toasting" (or rapping) over instrumental versions of other people's records, and then graduated to making records of their own. Others were more conventional "bands"—Black Uhuru, the group that brought Michael Rose, Don Carlos, and Sly and Robbie to mainstream prominence, were (and remain) one of the greatest roots bands of all time.

One thing that almost all of them had in common was the burning rage of righteousness: a need to ensure that social injustices were confronted head-on and cultural ills were torn to shreds. Another was that they all worked with, or listened to, Lee Perry.

Perry had been around the Jamaican scene since the late 1950s, when he worked briefly as a songwriter for Duke Reid. That relationship shattered following one argument to many; and Perry skipped across town to Coxsone Dodd's Studio One, initially as an errand boy but quickly rising to head of A&R where he oversaw the Sunday afternoon auditions that Dodd staged every week at his Orange Street store.

Perry also recorded in his own right; and in 1959 he released his debut single, "Old for New," on Dodd's Coxsone label. He followed up by championing a new popular dance called the "Chicken Scratch," a title that became the inspiration behind the best known of Perry's nicknames. He would forever be referred to as Scratch.

Perry was an integral part of the Studio One setup, producing and/or writing for an impressive slew of artists: **Delroy Wilson**, the Maytals, the Wailers, **Shenley Duffus**, and many more. He unleashed, too, a string of memorable singles of his own, including two of the greatest slabs of danceable lewdness ever hatched, "Doctor Dick" and "Rub and Squeeze," both of which were recorded with the future **Rita Marley**'s vocal group, **the Soulettes**. Then, turning freelance following a break with Studio One in 1966, he engineered sessions by Prince Buster, JJ Johnson, and others at the WIRL studios, often accepting payment in further studio time. The gems "Run for Cover," "Whup Whup Man," and "Set Them Free" duly followed.

By 1967, Perry was working for producer **Joe Gibbs**, and setting in motion another wave of new talent. He discovered **the Versatiles** and inaugurated a long relationship with their frontman **Junior Byles**. He produced hits by **Errol Dunkley**, **Errol Brown**, and the ever-fabulous **Pioneers**, and even found the time to earn another lasting nickname as well, taken from the title of his next hit single, "The Upsetter."

Perry's early recordings, like his productions, rarely sounded like anybody else. Already in possession of a most distinctive voice, he delighted in melding it to equally distinctive rhythmic tricks and sound effects. And if his own records could be strange, what he did to other artists' was positively bizarre. The B-side of **Burt Walters**'s "Honey Love," for instance, reprised the A-side with the vocal played backward over the backing track. Another, "Noisy Village," found him playing **the Tennors**' "Ride Me Donkey" at half speed, then layering it with bizarre sound effects.

TWELVE CRUCIAL LEE PERRY PRODUCTIONS OF THE 1970S

Prisoner of Love: Dave Barker Meets the Upsetters —Dave Barker (1970)

Possessor of one of the sweetest singing voices around, **Dave Barker** was also capable of some of the most violent yelping, and this primal set allows both sounds to reign supreme. Highlights include the signature "Shocks of Mighty," James Brown's "My Cup," the delirious "Prisoner of Love," and an absolutely outrageous assault on Dylan's "Blowin' in the Wind."

Beat Down Babylon—Junior Byles (1973)

If ever there was a match made in heaven, it was the day Perry and Byles first came together in a studio and began the partnership that would culminate in this record. Byles's debut album is a masterpiece of dread lyricism and foreboding spiritualism, while Perry's production sees him pressing any number of odd devices into essential play—a whip cracking through the title track, a machine gun rattling across "Coming Home." Caution: *two* geniuses at work.

Silver Bullets—The Silvertones (1973)

The Silvertones were already established as one of the quintessential vocal groups of the 1960s, but Perry ensured their magic persisted into the new decade too. Low on craziness but high on sweetness, songs like "Early in the Morning," "Souvenir of Mexico," and "Rejoice Jah Jah Children" catch all concerned effortlessly re-harnessing past glories.

Musical Bones—Vin Gordon (1973)

As **Don Drummond Jr.**, **Vin Gordon** was one of Jamaica's busiest session musicians, a trombonist *par excellence* who was rarely given the opportunity to shine outside of other people's recordings. Perry granted him that luxury, and this album justifies his faith.

Natty Passing Through—Prince Jazzbo (1976)

Prince Jazzbo was one of the mid-1970s' most volatile toasters, which means his union with Perry was the musical equivalent to nuclear fission. Play loud and stand back.

Hurt So Good—Susan Cadogan (1976)

The Perry-produced title track became a massive U.K. hit in 1975, but British record company politics saw his other recordings with librarian **Susan Cadogan** shelved, while a new album, the slippery ***Doing It Her Way***, was pushed out instead. It took a year for this set to materialize, to prove it should have been out there all along. Her version of "In the Ghetto" is heartbreakingly sincere; "Don't You Burn Your Bridges" is painfully admonitory; and no praise on Earth is too high for "Hurt So Good."

Party Time—The Heptones (1976)

A sheer wonder, as the Heptones revisit their golden oldie "Crying Over

You" and wind up with the definitive version, and then turn around and follow it with "Mr. President" and the truly incendiary "Sufferer's Time."

War ina Babylon—Max Romeo (1976)

Max Romeo is certainly one of the key figures in Jamaican music, with a career that made significant contributions to everything from the vocal-group scene of the mid-1960s through to the rude-reggae boom as the decades turned over. By the early 1970s, however, he was delving deep into his political consciousness, a process that climaxed with this—both a song and an album that crystallize roots rebellion for all the ages.

Police and Thieves—Junior Murvin (1977)

Spawning covers from as far afield as the Clash and Boy George, the title track is such a part of the furniture that it's easy to forget that there's a whole album of similar quality behind it. In fact, this would have been one of the crucial roots albums even without "Police and Thieves," as "Lucifer," "Rescue Jah Children," and the seething *nyahbinghi* "Working in a Cornfield" all match the hit for intensity, while Murvin's vocals are a thing of wonder in their own right.

Super Eight—George Faith (1977)

Another album that would probably be overlooked completely were Perry's name not attached to it. But that would be a big mistake. Titled for the fact it contains just eight tracks (and all are super), **George Faith**'s *Super Eight* is constructed to almost Spector-esque proportions, and includes versions of "In the Midnight Hour" and "Diana" that will completely rewire your brain.

Heart of the Congos—The Congos (1977)

Unerringly constructed around Cedric Myton's angelic falsetto, easing in and around **the Congos**' deep roots sonics, this could well be Perry's best-ever work, an album that allows his own creativity full rein without ever stepping on the toes of the music. There are no highlights on this album—the whole thing is dynamite.

***Conscious Man*—The Jolly Brothers (1993)**

Incredibly, it took some sixteen years for this album to be released. A classic 1977–1978 Black Ark production, it was shelved when the various **Jolly Brothers** fell out over which direction to pursue: a pop-oriented angle suggested by recordings they'd made with **Prince Jammy** or the foreboding roots that Perry pulled from their 1978 hit single "Conscious Man." The Jammy stuff won, and that was the end of the Jolly Brothers.

But he had the ear of the dance floor, both at home and abroad. "Return of Django" was a British Top 5 hit; while "Ten to Twelve," "Night Doctor" (one of the first records ever to feature drummer Sly Dunbar), "(Dangerous) Man from MI5," and "Medical Operation" were all Jamaican hits. His productions, too, were unstoppable, as **Slim Smith** (an ex-member of the Techniques and **the Uniques**), Dave Barker (later of the British chart-topping duo Dave and Ansel Collins), **Busty Brown**, **Winston Jarrett**, the Silvertones, the Bleechers, and Nora Dean all emerged with solid-gold singles.

He accompanied Bob Marley and the Wailers through two albums of vital music; helped launch the careers of toasters **Dennis Alcapone** and Prince Winston Thompson (the future **Dr. Alimantado**); and drew Junior Byles out of the confines of the Versatiles to become one of the era's most remarkable solo performers. And in 1973, Perry purchased a house and spent the next six months converting its backyard into what became the most legendary studios of the age, the Black Ark.

Compared to other studios around town, it was a very rudimentary operation, largely constructed from more-or-less obsolete equipment purchased from other producers as they upgraded. But Black Ark had one thing that no other studio could offer: Perry's ingenuity. Any modern compilation of Black Ark–era Perry will abound with invention and even madness, for there was no holding back either his ambition or the fruits of his labors.

Black Ark handled everything. Massive pop hits like **Leo**

Graham's "Black Candle," Junior Byles's **"Curly Locks,"** and Susan Cadogan's "Hurt So Good" were joined by crucial cuts by toasters Dillinger, **I-Roy**, and **Charlie Ace**; earthshaking dub collaborations with **Niney Holness** and **King Tubby**; and some of the most vital roots music of the age.

It was Perry who oversaw Jamaican music's transition from an almost exclusively 45s-driven market to one that at least acknowledged the importance of LPs, which in turn helped popularize the music with overseas audiences. Particularly when they were confronted with albums the quality of Byles's *Beat Down Babylon*, Junior Murvin's *Police and Thieves*, the Congos' *Heart of the Congos*, and Max Romeo's *War ina Babylon*. Clarion calls for the roots explosion, these albums remain as electrifying today as they were at the time. Perry reunited with Bob Marley for sessions that bled into the ongoing sessions for the *Exodus* album, and included the semi-legendary "Punky Reggae Party," a celebration written by Marley after Perry told him of his experiences producing the British punk band the Clash.

Neither were these the peak of Perry's roots productions. There was a string of singles, equally powerful, equally quintessential: **the Unforgettables**' "Many a Call," Lee Locks's "What Can I Do," **Bunny and Rickie**'s "Too Bad Bull," and **Prince Jazzbo**'s "Penny Reel"; and, of course, Perry's own output, spread across such albums as ***Return of Wax***, ***Kung Fu Meets the Dragon***, ***Roast Fish Collie Weed and Corn Bread***, ***Super Ape***, and ***Return of the Super Ape***.

All are indispensable; all are nigh-on indescribable. But nobody should be without *Return of the Super Ape*, an album that boasts some of the heaviest dubs of Perry's career, but also some of the most pop-inflected and simultaneously atmospheric music too. The precise point where earth rhythm and heavenly inspiration meet and melt together, *Return of the Super Ape* conjoins jazz riffs with punk and R&B, and gospel harmony with barking-mad breaks of unimagined savagery.

Storm clouds were gathering, however. Island Records inked a deal to carry Perry output to an international audience, and then began quibbling over the quality of some of his work, including several of his own albums and—incredibly—the Congos LP, a magnificent accomplishment whose legendary status has not been denied by anyone who has heard it. Certainly Perry could not believe what he was being told; and if these decisions were being made on musical terms, neither could anyone else. But a growing reliance on alcohol and marijuana had further fueled Perry's reputation for unpredictability; and slowly, both Black Ark and his work within deteriorated. When fire destroyed the studio in 1983, it was the end of an era, although Perry-watchers insisted that the end had actually come four or five years earlier.

Perry slipped into twilight, that shadowy realm in which all-pervasive legend elbowed reality to the curb. It was said that he lived amid the charred ruins of the studio for a time, worshipping bananas and baptizing visitors with his garden hose. And while he remained musically active, little of his work through the 1980s could hold a candle to that he had been machine-gunning out a few years earlier.

His relationship with Island finally crumbled when Perry declared label head Chris Blackwell responsible for Bob Marley's death, and accused him of vampirism in the song "Judgement inna Babylon." It would be 1987 before another truly great Scratch album arrived, a union with British dub maestro **Adrian Sherwood** titled ***Time Boom X de Devil Dead***.

Since that time, and with one hand now knowingly grasping his reputation for madness and more, Perry has reestablished himself as one of the greatest entertainers on the reggae circuit, his regular live shows and occasional albums maybe not recapturing the alchemy that was once his musical lifeblood, but certainly showing us all where it came from. Catch ***Return from Planet Dub***, featuring Perry making madness with Austria's Dubblestandart and a host of likeminded souls—**Ari Up**, David Lynch, and Gudrun among them. The Upsetter is still upsetting.

The harder they come … and Jimmy Cliff was the hardest. (Author's collection)

7

THREE WISE MEN: JIMMY CLIFF, GREGORY ISAACS, AND DENNIS BROWN

JIMMY CLIFF

Many artists have, via a selection of well-chosen covers or an ability to kangaroo themselves through changing styles, served up what could be called a one-stop guide to the history of reggae as it marched from ska onward. The British band **UB40** alone have released three volumes of ***Labour of Love***, covering favorite songs of those eras, and there are others.

Few, however, have looked beyond those periods in search of a chronology to cover. It is therefore fitting that of those that have, the most successful is Jimmy Cliff, a man whose own career takes us back to the very birth of ska in the early 1960s and is still going strong half a century later in 2012.

Indeed, Cliff's latest album, ***Rebirth*** (and the accompanying ***Sacred Fire*** EP) is arguably his most dynamic since the run of early 1970s discs that established him as Jamaica's first international pop star. Dramatically produced by **Tim Armstrong** of the American band Rancid, Cliff's eye for the music's heritage did not stop with borders-bashing covers of the British Clash's "Guns of Brixton" and Rancid's "Ruby Soho." The song "Reggae Music" is itself the story of Cliff's own career, taking him back to the fifteen-year-old who in 1962 cut his first single, "Daisy Got Me Crazy," and tracing the music's evolution hand in hand with his own.

Reggay, or reggae, was more than a fashionable new dance, more than a simple shift in tempo and beat. Or, at least, it became more. Swiftly adopted as the generic name under which all Jamaican musical forms would henceforth be grouped, the birth of reggae ushered in an era of unparalleled musical experimentation and untrammeled sonic curiosity, an age in which the complex harmonies of one band and the jerking hyperactivity of another could fall side by side onto the turntable or off a compilation, and still be described by the same single word.

It was reggae that truly brought Jamaican music into the international arena, and that was the charge that Cliff was destined to lead.

Cliff was already a Jamaican chart veteran when the anthemic "Wonderful World, Beautiful People" brought him his debut American hit in 1969, but such plaudits counted for little at the time. It would be Cliff's present and future, not his past, that allowed him to throw open the door through which a host of other Jamaican artists would pour over the next few years. Prior to Cliff's emergence, reggae artists spoke to reggae fans alone. But Cliff appealed across the board.

"Wonderful World, Beautiful People" was followed into the chart by "Vietnam," an antiwar number that Bob Dylan (himself no slouch when it came to such things) described as the best protest song he'd ever heard. The ***Wonderful World*** album opened up to reveal the beauties "Come into My Life" and "Hard Road to Travel," both evincing a versatility that made his Jamaican heritage seem almost irrelevant. Rather, just as Curtis Mayfield was encouraged to place his R&B leanings behind him and target his music (or, at least, his marketing) at the predominantly white, middle-class market for singer-songwriters, so Cliff, too, found himself being offered up to the crowds garnered by the other great troubadours of the age: James Taylor, Cat Stevens, the newly solo Paul Simon, and (the young, pre-spectacular-spectacles) Elton John.

That linkage was only strengthened when Cliff covered Cat Stevens's "Wild World" for his next hit single (the Cat produced the record); then, again, when both Paul Simon and Elton John traveled to Kingston, Jamaica, to record with the same producer, musicians, and studio as Cliff had utilized on his hits. Simon's "Mother and Child Reunion" is not *great* reggae. But it is reggae all the same.

"Wild World" was still riding the charts when another Cliff composition, "You Can Get It If You Really Want It," brought Desmond Dekker a massive hit during the summer of 1970. And while the death of Cliff's longtime producer Leslie Kong in August 1971 slowed the singer's momentum, his next singles—the contemplative lament of "Sitting In Limbo" and "Struggling Man"—were effortlessly the equals of anything else in the so-called singer-songwriter genre.

Neither was Cliff prone to the same career mistakes as certain of his contemporaries. Arguably, neither James Taylor (acting in the movie *Two-Lane Blacktop*) nor Cat Stevens (soundtracking *Harold and Maude*) offered anything more to their ongoing careers than a mild diversion when they turned their attentions to the movie screen.

Cliff, however, grasped the opportunity with both hands. Cast in the lead role of the movie *The Harder They Come*, a gritty portrayal of lowlife on the streets of Kingston, he astonished all comers with his portrayal of a young musical hopeful struggling against the Kingston music industry's gangland-style corruption. Neither did his contribution end there. Adding his voice to the movie's soundtrack, he gifted it with two of his greatest-ever songs, the yearning, near-gospel flavored "Many Rivers to Cross," and the truly magnificent "The Harder They Come" itself.

It was the peak of his career, at least until the so aptly titled *Rebirth* came along. Future Cliff albums neither matched nor repeated the warm brilliance of his early 1970s output. But he continued recording, continued scoring hits, and continued influencing generation after generation not only of reggae artists, but singer-songwriters of every musical persuasion. Far from being recalled as Jamaica's first international superstar, it is more accurate to regard him as its most enduring, as well.

GREGORY ISAACS

Cliff was not the only silver-tongued Jamaican singer to make major inroads into the American mainstream market as the 1970s rolled on. The late Gregory Isaacs, too, saw his Jamaican success reflected here, courtesy of what his admirers still describe as the sweetest voice in reggae music: an easing, smoothing seduction that holds hearts captive long enough to reach into their soul, and captures souls for just enough time to make their hearts burst with its beauty. And neither time nor familiarity can ever dull its majesty. The classics "Night Nurse" and "All I Have Is Love" were long ago confined to the land of golden oldies, but both still sound as fresh today as they did the first time.

THE TROJAN STORY

Of all the record labels that have brought Jamaican music to the international masses, none holds a more sainted place in the heart of fans than Trojan Records. Not only did the label itself score more European hit singles than all of its competitors put together, it also handled the international output of dozens of other, smaller, Jamaican labels, each of which was pumping out records at a rate that today's music industry simply couldn't imagine, and scoring hits with many of them. And it offered up something else. A guarantee that no matter whether you had heard of an artist or not, if a record was on Trojan, it was going to be great.

Trojan was run by Lee Gopthal, a veteran of the British ska scene; at one point in the early 1960s, he owned the London office where Island Records got their start. Indeed, it was Island's decision to move away from Jamaican music (their original forte) in favor of rockier underground sounds in 1967 that prompted the birth of Trojan, a point that was pressed home with suitable force on one of the 1997 compilations released to celebrate the fortieth anniversary of Island's founding.

Ska Island was a fifteen-track retrospective anchored firmly in the present to give perspective on the past. Recruiting names and songs from across the music's history, it paired old-school performers with new, then unleashed them all on some of the genre's best-loved classics.

Prince Buster opened things up, teaming up with the Skatalites for a solid workout through Desmond Dekker's "King of Kings"; at the other end of the spectrum, latter-day heroes **the Trojans** wrapped themselves around **Jackie Edwards**'s "Keep On Running" (the song that gave the

Spencer Davis Group an international chart-topper in the mid-1960s); and in between times, **Fishbone**, the Toasters, vintage hornman **Rico Rodriguez**, venerable veteran **Laurel Aitken**, **Hepcat**, and **the Determinations** jumped in with their own takes on the musical form, which has been through multitudinous changes since it first appeared, but has always remained true to itself.

Island was going to be a hard act to follow, then. But Trojan was up to the task. Over the next few years, deals were struck with every Jamaican producer that Island had dealt with, then expanded to include almost everybody else. And so Trojan exploded. Soon, the label boasted over forty different named subsidiaries, some of which survived for just a handful of singles, but many of which enjoyed incredible life spans. Throughout the late 1960s and 1970s, Trojan's universe was boundless. And so was the litany of success that it conjured up.

Jimmy Cliff was Trojan's major star, with Toots and the Maytals and Judge Dread coming in a close second. Bob Marley and the Wailers had been Trojan artists before they joined Island, and so had Lee Perry. Beyond them, however, few of Trojan's best-remembered acts actually enjoyed lengthy careers outside of their homeland. Rather, the one-hit wonder was the rule. Jimmy Cliff aside, only Desmond Dekker (whose records, ironically, were originally released on the rival President label) comprehensively bucked that trend. The worldwide monster "The Israelites" followed on from "007 (Shanty Town)" and preceded the mighty "It Mek," while "Pickney Girl" and "You Can Get It If You Really Want It" ensured Dekker's star would remain aloft.

But ex-Upsetters vocalist Dave Barker and his new partner, Ansel Collins, also enjoyed more than a single moment of glory. Not only did Dave and Ansel grab a British #1 with "Double Barrel," they promptly followed it up with the heavy, heavy monster sound of "Monkey Spanner."

Back in Jamaica, the music scene was already shifting toward a heavier roots vibe. But across Europe, it was the immediately danceable sounds that scored the highest, classics like the Upsetters' "Return of Django"; **the Harry J All Stars**' "The Liquidator"; **the Pioneers**' "Long Shot (Kick de Bucket)" (an ode to a legendary Jamaican racehorse); **Greyhound**'s "Black and White"; and many more. Hits by **Ken Boothe**, John Holt, and **Bob and Marcia** were as familiar in the kitchens of suburbia as they were in the dancehalls of the cities, while the budget-priced ***Tighten Up*** series of compilation albums soundtracked the generation that grew up to become the 2-Tone scene a decade later.

That debt was repaid when the 2-Tone bands stashed a veritable sound system's worth of covers into their early live sets: the Skatalites' "Guns of Navarone," **Tony Tribe**'s "Red Red Wine," **Symarip**'s "Skinhead Moonstomp," and "Double Barrel" all reverberated across the U.K. ska scene of the late 1970s. And it wasn't only the post-punk movement that toyed with Trojan's reputation. John Lennon and Harry Nilsson recorded Jimmy Cliff's "Many Rivers to Cross"; German disco sensation Boney M. and American Linda Ronstadt both covered **the Melodians**' "Rivers of Babylon." The Rolling Stones re-created **Eric Donaldson**'s "Cherry Oh Baby," and both **Barry Biggs** and **Boris Gardiner**, early Trojan stars, were having hits well into the new decade. Their longevity alone would be tribute enough to Trojan's impact and importance, but the story did not end there.

Revitalized in the mid-1980s and leaping wholeheartedly into the CD-reissue boom, Trojan became one of the principal players on the reggae scene once again, courtesy not only of a series of well-stuffed single-artist compilations that brought together more forgotten 45s than even hardcore collectors could hope to hear, but also of a fifty-plus series of three-CD box sets devoted to every theme the marketing men could conceive. Two label-spanning box sets, too, testify to Trojan's magical output (2011's *The Trojan Records Story* delivers five discs of musical ecstasy); the company's history has been recorded in an excellent book by author Laurence Cane-Honeysett; and still eBay resounds to the sound of record-breaking purchases.

Trojan is not merely a record label. It is a hallmark of quality.

The Cool Ruler, the original Mr. Loverman, Isaacs had also been dominating his homeland music scene for a decade by the time American audiences caught up with him. Discovered by the legendary producer **Alvin Ranglin**, his first big hit was the wholly self-defining "Love Is Overdue," a stunning performance that would set the scene for every great record Isaacs had in him, yearning, pleading, and implausibly intimate. Isaacs's personal life may have been a tumultuous cavalcade of drugs and jail, but place him behind a microphone and he could charm the cherries from between your knees.

Success was not slow in finding him, at home or abroad. By the late 1970s, Isaacs was arguably the biggest reggae performer in the world, up there alongside Dennis Brown (with whom he frequently toured and duetted) and Bob Marley, and outselling them both in the reggae market. Indeed, his African Museum label was itself responsible for releasing some of Brown's own greatest records, but it was Isaacs's output that people kept their ears out for the most.

Early hits like "Loving Pauper," "Lonely Lover," "Promised Land," and "My Only Lover"; later successes like "Permanent Lover" and "Wish You Were Mine"; timeless gems like "Let Love In," a dynamic duet with Brown included on the pair's so-aptly titled ***Two Bad Superstars*** album—these were the records that established Isaacs's reputation, and having established it, kept it at the top.

Isaacs wasn't simply a romancer, though. He also maintained a stream of political consciousness, and performed from the same role of dogged underdoggery that fueled his lovers' laments, biting all the harder for that: "Financial Endorsement," "Rasta Business," "Village of the Under Privileged," "The Philistines." And then, of course, there was "Night Nurse," which Isaacs recorded with that most fabulous of backing bands, the **Roots Radics**, and which reggae historian Lloyd Bradley once said made women go so weak that "the guys would hold them up that little bit tighter. For the full three minutes." And when he died on October 25, 2010, more than one obituarist reckoned the lights had gone out on lovers rock.

DENNIS BROWN

Dennis Brown, too, enjoyed a career that was dominated by highs and highlights; so much so that singling out any individual moment as most worthy of attention seems like a fool's errand. But then you hear his performance at the Montreux Festival in 1979, and everything that established the self-styled Crown Prince Emmanuel among Jamaica's greatest exports comes rushing into view.

Brown himself was at an all-time peak. The previous year, he had reunited with producer Joe Gibbs to re-spark a relationship that dated back to the dawn of Brown's singing career. Their first album together, 1978's *Visions*, promptly unleashed two massive hit singles, "Equal Rights" and "How Can I Leave," while Brown also proved one of the runaway successes at both the epochal One Love Peace Concert at Kingston's National Stadium and the inaugural Reggae Sunsplash Festival.

It was the duo's revival of Brown's early hit "Money in My Pocket" that cemented the international acclaim, however. Rerecorded for 1979's ***Words of Wisdom*** album, the song was already a long-established classic—in fact, it was one of the first songs he ever recorded with Joe Gibbs, at the producer's Duhaney Park studio. With engineer Niney Holness also at his side, the sixteen-year-old Brown laid down one of the all-time greats, only to supersede even that spectacular performance when he returned to the song seven years later.

"Money in My Pocket" took the British Top 20 by storm in March 1979, and was soon heading chart-ward across Europe as well. Even before the show, it was clear that the Montreux Festival performance was going to send his star even higher, and so it proved. By 1981, Brown and Gibbs had procured a major-label deal, and were cutting the two albums that would establish the singer as Jamaica's first new superstar since the death of Bob Marley. It was a mantle that Brown would retain for the remainder of his life.

Born in 1957, Dennis Brown grew up on Kingston's Orange Street, one of the myriad kids who spent their days watching and listening as the biggest stars of the age marched back and forth to the recording studios that flourished around the neighborhood. Brown was not the only one who vowed that one day, he would be making that same journey himself—but he was one of the few who truly succeeded at such.

By the age of eleven, in 1968, Brown was recording with legendary producer Coxsone Dodd, scoring a Jamaican hit with a cover of the Impressions' "No Man Is an Island." A string of further singles with Dodd (and, later, Prince Buster) kept Brown in the spotlight. They also evinced a talent that, unlike those possessed by so many other child stars of the age, was not going to dissipate as time went by.

By 1972, Brown had recorded with virtually every major name producer in Kingston; and at every fresh port of call, he demonstrated his versatility and skill by turning his talents to whichever song the producers demanded. From the country lament "Wichita Linesman" and onto a magnificent rendering of the Fleetwood Mac/Santana classic "Black Magic Woman," Brown's abilities were truly without peer. (Or shame. Sometimes, listening to the AOR-pop garbage he occasionally turned to, you really wondered what was going through his mind. The lightweight pap of "Little Green Apples," I'm talking to you.)

It was his work with Gibbs and Holness, however, that dictated the course of Brown's immediate future, all the more so after he and Holness broke away in 1973 to record the string of electrifying roots rockers that kept Brown jumping across the next two years. The electrifying "Westbound Train," "Have No Fear," "Cassandra," "Go Now," "No More Will I Roam," "I Am the Conqueror," "Ride On Ride On" (a devastating duet with toaster **Big Youth**), "Africa," and "Tribulation" were all major hits. When Bob Marley described Brown as the best reggae singer in the world, he did so confident that the youth was only going to get better.

Marley was correct. Brown's Montreux repertoire jangles with classics. The opening "So Jah Say" was another Joe Gibbs special; so was his cover of the old Alton Ellis masterpiece "Ain't That Loving You." "Wolf and Leopards" was the Holness-produced title cut from what was then his best-known album; "Whip Them Jah" had just become a hit for the second time. "How Can I Leave" was a cover of an old **Sharks**' hit that was about to bring Brown yet another Jamaican smash; "Words of Wisdom," of course, had named his most recent album. From start to the inevitable finish, a triumphant "Money in My Pocket," the concert was vintage Dennis Brown, played out in front of an audience that may have only known the big hit as it made its way into the venue, but was certainly dancing to a different tune by the time the concert ended.

Brown remained alongside Joe Gibbs until 1983, by which time his own musical attention was being drawn away from the international success he had so recently won and back to the Jamaican grassroots scene. Entranced by the dancehall explosion, Brown was an active patron and participant, working alongside the likes of new stars **Brigadier Jerry**, Sammy Dread, and **Michael Prophet**, even as he continued recording in his traditional vein. Indeed, such was his appetite for work that, over the next fifteen years, Brown was regularly releasing up to six different albums' worth of material every year. When Brown rounded off the 1980s with an album titled ***Unchallenged***, few people would have even dreamed of contradicting that claim.

1991 saw Brown sing alongside **Twitch** and **Brian and Tony Gold** for the dancehall smashes "Hypocrite Corner" and "Poison"; 1992's ***Blazing*** album brought Brown voice-to-voice with **Shabba Ranks** and **Maxi Priest** for a red-hot "Fever." Behind the scenes, and certainly unbeknownst to his still-dedicated international following, however, Brown was in trouble. He had long been nursing a serious cocaine habit; and, on July 1, 1999, he was raced to a Kingston hospital emergency room, unconscious and suffering from a collapsed lung, a direct result of his drug use. He died while the doctors were attempting to re-inflate it.

News of Brown's passing hit the reggae world hard, with consolation drawn only from the knowledge that the singer's insatiable appetite for the studio and the stage had bequeathed a musical legacy that will live forever. The magical Montreux concert is a vital part of that bequest.

Keith Richards—Wingless Angel and Rolling Stone.
(Paramount Classics/Photofest)

8

KEITH RICHARDS'S WINGLESS ANGELS: SKANKING WITH THE STONES

When the Rolling Stones arrived in Kingston, Jamaica, in November 1972 to begin work on their next album, few knew what to expect. The city's leading studio, Dynamic Sounds, was enjoying an utterly unexpected moment in the sun; and as a growing trickle of British and American musicians came over to check it out, each one raised the setup's profile a little higher. The Stones, however, were about as big as anyone could be, decade-old survivors of Britain's early-sixties beat boom whose insistence that they were the greatest rock 'n' roll band in the world was being echoed by almost everyone who heard it.

Keith Richards was the driving force behind the decision to head to Kingston, and it was his musical tastes that informed it, even though all were adamant that the Stones did not intend to make a reggae album. Rather, they wanted to create something that was informed by the attitudes and freedom of reggae.

But there were more practical reasons too, as Richards admitted in the coffee-table-crushing *According to the Rolling Stones* in 2002. "Jamaica was one of the few places that would let us all in! By that time, about the only country that I was allowed to exist in was Switzerland, which was damn boring for me, at least for the first year, because I didn't like to ski ... Nine countries kicked me out, thank you very much, so it was a matter of how to keep this thing together."

With the musicians and entourage settled in and around Kingston, the recording sessions kicked off with a version of

"Winter," a slow burner that would make the finished album, the immortally titled *Goats Head Soup*. And by the time the operation left the island in December, the LP's final track listing was already in place. But there was a lot of material left behind too, songs like "Waiting for a Friend," which would ultimately be polished up for the *Tattoo You* album in 1981; the storming "You Should Have Seen Her Ass"; the chunky "Criss Cross Man"; and so many more. None of which, true to the group's insistence, owed much more than a certain smoky atmosphere to the Stones' surroundings.

Dancing at the back of Richards's mind, however, were a couple of songs that went considerably further. Rehearsal tapes recorded at his Longview Farm home earlier in 1972 feature the guitarist alone playing around with a supremely loose-limbed version of Jamaican singer Eric Donaldson's falsetto showcase "Cherry Oh Baby." He toyed, too, with one of his own compositions, a lightweight but nevertheless reggae-tinged "I Can Feel the Fire," a number that he would eventually donate to future Stone **Ron Wood**'s first solo album.

"Cherry Oh Baby" was not just a passing fancy, either. It was destined to become the Stones' first serious stab at playing reggae, and arguably their most successful, at least until Richards alone tackled Jimmy Cliff's "The Harder They Come" for a 1978 solo single—turning in a desperate, almost wasted-sounding plea for understanding and compassion.

Lacking, though it did, the weighty reverb with which mainstream reggae was already becoming fascinated (a failing that "The Harder They Come" would more than compensate for); hamstrung though it was by the Bill Wyman/Charlie Watts rhythm section's apparent uncertainty over the exact nature of reggae's trademark offbeat, "Cherry Oh Baby"'s very lack of studied sophistication was its saving grace. Whereas Eric Clapton could be accused of having taken reggae music, then developed his own unique style around it, the Stones took the opposite approach entirely.

They knew (and they still knew four years later, when they sent the whole thing up with *Emotional Rescue*'s "Send Her to Me") that (collectively, at least) they would never play reggae like the Rastafarians. So they didn't even make the attempt, and they ended up coming closer to the spirit of the genre than even they have given themselves credit for.

Black and Blue, the 1976 album that would house "Cherry Oh Baby," is often described (and not always politely) as the Stones' disco album, and there is some truth to that. What, after all, was disco if not the latest convolution of the same R&B music that the Stones had set out to play in 1962? It was not as though they exactly threw themselves into tight white trousers and posed beneath a mirror ball.

Outtakes from the album (like so much of *Goats Head Soup*'s unused ingredients) find the band relaxing into any number of riffs and rhythms, and doing so with an eye for any danceable sound, be it funk, disco, or indeed reggae. In fact, one of the manifold bootlegs that preserve the sessions is pointedly titled ***Reggae 'n' Roll***, and arrives replete with a sprawling, skanking instrumental title track that simply cries out for lyrics (and maybe a remix). Add the moods and momentum that lays across fellow loose ends "Sexy Nites," "Travellin' Man," and "Man Eating Woman," and had the Stones' ultimate intentions only moved in the right direction, *Black and Blue* could have been a very different album altogether.

No matter. Reggae was now an established component of the band's musical arsenal, both on record and beyond. They took Black Uhuru on tour with them in 1982, at a time when that band's popularity approached even the Wailers' levels; and they signed Peter Tosh to their Rolling Stones Records label, and gifted him with his first international hit single, a duet with Mick Jagger across the old Temptations number "(You Gotta Walk) Don't Look Back." And 1983's "Undercover of the Night" became the first of many Stones singles to be made available with a dub-remix B-side, and the deep-dish dynamism with which this document of urban collapse was delivered stands among their mightiest latter-day achievements.

The true spirit of the Stones' reggae bloodlines, however, would remain a private concern for close to two decades more. Also in 1972, Keith Richards purchased a home in Ocho Rios; and for as long as he had lived there, he had been intrigued by *nyahbinghi*, the mélange of tribal percussion, strummed offbeat guitars, and voices raised in triumphant exultation that the mainstream music biz had more or less totally ignored—but that was the true soul and heartbeat of reggae in all its guises.

Richards's own fascination with the music is equally instinctive. *Nyahbinghi* music, he explained, was as close to spiritual purity as art could ever venture, a journey to a place where you forgot all the cares and suffering in the world and simply communed with the music itself. It was not long at all before he started playing with it, as bassist and producer **Brian Jobson** explains.

"Keith linked up with these guys who lived just down the road, and he'd go down and play with them and record it on cassettes. Every time he came back, he'd do that, and he really didn't think about it in terms of doing anything formal; it was just a lark, basically. But it really sounded good, and there was nothing else out there like that."

FIVE PRIMAL *NYAHBINGHI* ALBUMS (PLUS TWO COMPILATIONS)

Grounation—Count Ossie and the Mystic Revelation of Rastafari (1973)

Across six sides of vinyl (but at just eighty-three minutes) **Count Ossie and the Mystic Revelation of Rastafari** re-create a full grounation, its contents ranging from the honking jazz of "Bongo Man" to the side-long percussion-driven "Grounation," all of it cut through with the oratory of Brother Samuel Clayton. Recognizable to the uninitiated will be a version of the Folkes Brothers' "Oh Carolina," jazzer Charles Lloyd's "Mabrat," and the Jazz Crusaders' "Way Back," and there are definitely moments when the whole thing gets way too jazzy. But this is not the place to play "name that tune" or point accusing fingers at the horn section. It is a place to lay back and feel yourself transported.

Dadawah—Peace & Love—Ras Michael and the Sons of Negus (1975)

Just four tracks empower this album, the best of **Ras Michael and the Sons of Negus's** many releases, and certainly the one least informed by the group's interests in other musical forms.

The Light of Saba in Reggae—The Light of Saba (1978)

A hit single in the form of the then-little-known dub-poet **Mutabaruka**'s "Outcry" was many people's introduction to **the Light of Saba**'s most remarkable album; and while it might well prove a little too song-oriented for the true aficionado, it remains a vital offering.

Churchical Chants of the Nyahbinghi (1983)

Recorded live at the Church of Jah Rastafari in Freeman's Hall, Trelawney, in April 1982, and released the following year by the U.S. Heartbeat label, *Churchical Chants of the Nyahbinghi* was edited down from some seven days of ceremony, and maybe the edit was just a little too ruthless. No track tops the six-minute mark, with some sliced down to three, and listeners cannot help but wonder what was left on the cutting-room floor. The power of *nyahbinghi* lies in its hypnotic, mantric repetition. Lose that, and you lose a lot of magic.

The Rastafari Elders—The Rastafari Elders (1990)

Recorded in a Washington, D.C, studio in 1990, but as haunting as any "authentic" field recording.

Grounation: The Indomitable Spirit of Rastafari —various artists (1999)

A budget-priced collection of *nyahbinghi*-shaped offerings drawn from the Trojan catalogue, a healthy taster for anybody uncertain about diving into the ultimate treat . . .

Trojan Nyahbinghi—various artists (2003)

Three CDs and fifty tracks come close to exhausting the Trojan archive, with offerings that include representative slices from most of the above, plus cuts by Garnett Silk, **Ronnie Davis**, Nora Dean, and **Cynthia Richards**, to name just a few. Not every inclusion falls within the strict musicological definitions of the music, and there is a huge hole where Prince Buster's early experiments should be. But this ambitious and adventurous collection is still a must for anyone wanting to truly delve deep.

No, there wasn't. Back in the early-to-mid-1970s, *nyahbinghi* outfits like Ras Michael and the Sons of Negus and Prince Buster's occasional collaborator Count Ossie did get their music out on the U.K. Trojan label, but it sold poorly, and primarily to the curious. The Wailers recorded the rolling, dreaming "Rastaman Chant," and there are live versions in circulation that go on for ten deathless minutes or more. But the years since then saw *nyahbinghi* shrink back into the hills and mountains, at least so far as the mass market was concerned. So Richards's efforts in that direction were, according to Jobson, simply "a labor of love." But he kept at it. "Years ago, the first Ras Michael albums, the Count Ossie albums, they were really good. That basic premise is what we wanted."

They achieved it. With Jobson editing hours and hours of tape down to a manageable, releasable form, the 1997 ***Wingless Angels*** CD may have been more or less overlooked by the world at large, but anyone who heard it could not help but be utterly captivated. But then the Stones machine started up again, hauling Richards away for months...years...at a time.

Jobson: "We had done the first one, and we kept saying, 'Man, we have so many more tunes, we should do more,' although we still weren't thinking about 'what is the next step?' You know, it was just let's get together and play, get into the studio and record it, and see what happens. But it's difficult to get everybody in the same place; plus, when we did that first one, the Stones weren't that active.

"But then they started, and when you start up that machine, you can imagine, it has a momentum of its own. Keith didn't come back to Jamaica for quite a long while. The Stones were on tour, and then he had other things; it was almost like he forgot he had his house in Jamaica. For five years, he didn't come back, so when he came back the next time everybody was raring to go. So he said, 'Okay, we'll do it again.'"

Original Angels Jobson, Locksley Whitlock, Maureen Fremantle, Warrin Williamson, and Milton Beckerd all rejoined the crew, together with vocalist **Justin Hinds**, one of *the* quintessential stars of the early Jamaican scene, and possessor of one of *the* quintessential voices.

"The second one was done under much better conditions than the first one," Jobson recalls. "The first album was done at Keith's house; this one was done at an actual studio just down the road. The first one was everyone sitting in Keith's living room with two mikes, but this one we recorded everybody...we all had individual mikes this time."

Some things didn't change, however. "We recorded everything live, and each song went on for about thirty minutes. It was amazing, we recorded it over three or four days; and a lot of it, if you really check it, is traditional stuff. A lot is adapted from the English hymnal. So we would be starting a song and I'd be, 'Oops, I think we did that on the last album.'"

Other material was provided by bandmate Fremantle. "Maureen, she writes and she's a really good arranger as well. She would bring stuff in; some we adapted. There's a lot of reggae songs, Curtis Mayfield songs that we changed...and it's like a tank starting up; it starts slowly and then it builds and builds. The tempos speed up and slow down, and then you'd say, 'Next tune,' and they'd start playing the same one, and it's, 'No, man, we just did that one.' 'Oh, yeah, yeah...' But everything we played, in all of them, there were at least ten or fifteen minutes when it was really magic."

Wingless Angels II was recorded in 2004, around the same time as Keith Richards finally cut a follow-up to that two-decade-old version of "The Harder They Come," an equally essential cover of Toots and the Maytals' "Pressure Drop" for release as a download-only single. The following March, however, the veteran Hinds passed away. Locksley Whitlock died a few months later, and all work on the album halted. (A third Angel, Jackie Ellis, has also since passed on.)

The project was shelved; the musicians moved on. "And then Keith said, 'Man, we need to get it out as a tribute.' But he was about to go out on tour with the Stones, and he said, 'I don't know if I can do it, so can you just deal with it?' Because you can't get anything done when they're on the road. But he came in when he could to do overdubs...

"We had a lot of editing to do, but it's so evocative. When we were mixing it in L.A., people would come to the studio and say, 'What the hell is that?' But every time I hear it, I have to smile because it takes me back to the sessions, remembering all the jokes that were going around."

Future plans for **the Wingless Angels** are being laid. The first album has already been reissued as part of a deluxe edition twinned with its successor, and with twenty minutes' worth of a wealth of documentary footage. Richards has even discussed the Angels taking flight live, with Justin Hinds's son **Jerome** filling his father's shoes. For now, though, we have the music, and it is as timeless as it ought to be. The angels have wings after all.

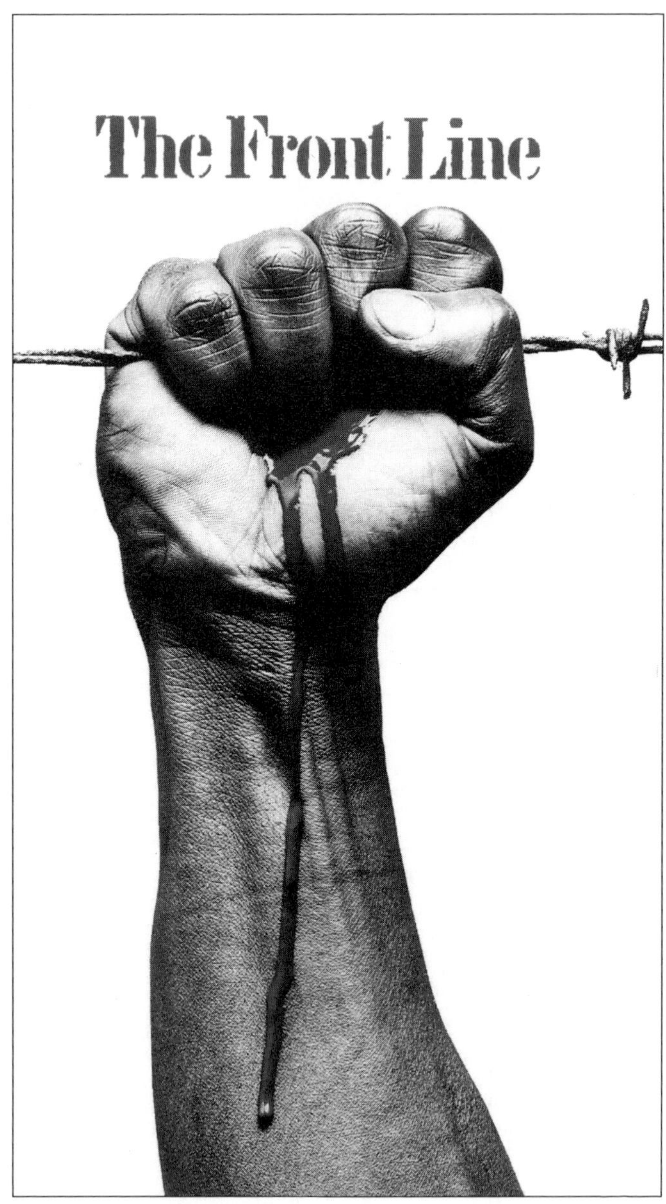

One of the most most powerful record company logos ever, for Virgin's redoubtable Front Line. (Author's collection)

9

SLAP SOME MORE ECHO ON IT: THE HEAVY, HEAVY MONSTER SOUND OF DUB

Dub is the sound of the heavens colliding, the final last frontier of dance music as it careens into any other genre it chooses. Rock, punk, electronics, and so many more have toyed, many times successfully, with the dub techniques that arose in the Jamaican studios of the late 1960s, often with results that can astonish even the most adept aficionado.

Bob Marley's own excursions into dub territory are few and far between. Famously, the Wailers' third album, the Lee Perry–produced ***Soul Revolution Part Two***, was released as a dub disc, although it was scarcely a shining example of either producer or artist's best work. Dig deeper into Marley and the Wailers' Jamaican 45s catalogue, or the *In Dub 1* compilation of both old and newly commissioned mixes, however, and some startling revisions emerge—although it must be said that the innate melody and message of Marley's work seldom permitted his music to undergo a thorough deconstruction. Because that is the true spirit of dub.

We begin by completely dismissing the modern marketing insistence that any kind of remix, particularly in the rock and R&B genres, is a dub mix. Dub is not simply a matter of twisting a few dials and making the bass a little louder, then adding a few funny noises. It is the absolute reconstruction of a piece of music, the stripping down of an existing song to its rawest rhythmic components for it then to be rebuilt into a completely different direction. A true dub doesn't simply stand apart from its counterpart. It is practically a whole new record.

The king of dub was, as his name suggested, the late King Tubby. In fact, to audiences raised on the reissues and retrospection of recent decades, King Tubby might as well *be* dub, so familiar is his name and so vast is his impact on the art. Far more than anybody else working in the dub arena of the 1970s and 1980s, Tubby took the music to its furthest reaches, sonically, technologically, and culturally. It is no exaggeration to say that several generations of future producers and dub-makers learned most of what they knew from King Tubby, if not in person, then by the shining example of his records.

King Tubby's first dubs, which in turn can be seen as the first dubs ever made, were created while he was employed as a disc-cutter at Duke Reid's Treasure Isle studios around 1968. It was becoming increasingly popular at the time for new singles to be backed by an instrumental version of the A-side (called, indeed, a "version"); not only did it cut down on the expense of having to record an actual B-side, it was also popular with disc jockeys, who could play the instrumental track and then perform their own lyrics or toasts over it.

One of Tubby's coworkers, engineer and sound-system operator "Ruddy" Redwood, had already taken to occasionally reworking some of these versions to emphasize the impact of the bass. Tubby, however, took it further than that. Far further. Yes, the bass would be amplified. But it would also be treated and tweaked, and around it the original tape would be halted, sped up, slowed down, and overdubbed with whatever sound effects were at hand. By the time he had finished, he had created a whole new performance.

His first dubs were for his personal use only. Tubby also operated a sound system, so he would press up a couple of acetates (or dub plates—the term was already in use before the genre was created) and spin them exclusively at his own shows. But soon, other disc jockeys were hearing what he did and, having determined that they could never compete with him in sonic terms, began commissioning their own dubs from Tubs. **U-Roy**, I-Roy, Big Youth, **Dean Beckford**, and Berry Simpson, all destined to become giants of the dancehall DJ scene, cut their toasting teeth on Tubby dub plates; and soon, other producers and engineers were getting their own efforts onto the dance floors too. Dub had arrived.

The best dubs, and therefore dubbers, were the most distinctive ones. By virtue of his already escalating reputation for sonic experimentation and dislocation, Lee Perry was an early entrant into the field, often employing dub techniques within the very creation of a new song, and then allowing the later dub side to stray even further afield.

Niney Holness and **Keith Hudson** followed. Before you even delve into remainder of his catalogue, dub variations of Niney's classic "Blood and Fire" are still capable of shaking the foundations of your record collection, while Hudson's dubs alone explain why he was known as "the Dark Prince of Reggae." Two astonishing dub albums, ***Pick a Dub*** (1974) and ***Brand*** (1977), played alongside the vocal sets ***Furnace*** (1972), ***Flesh of My Skin, Blood of My Blood*** (1974), and ***Rasta Communication*** (1978), testify to the sheer genius of Hudson's 1970s catalogue.

Meanwhile, Tubby's first bona fide Jamaican hit arrived in 1974. "Watergate Rock" was his dub interpretation of **Larry Marshall**'s "I Admire You"; and if the floodgates had already been opened by his earlier work, the success of this latest effort blew them off the hinges. Bunny Lee's King Tubby remix LP ***Dub from the Roots*** followed; then came ***Dubbing with the Observer***, a bruising collision between Tubby and Niney.

But perhaps the most important of them all, even more so than Tubby's 1977 masterpiece ***King Tubby Meets the Rockers Uptown***, was Rupie Edwards's 1974 masterpiece "Ire Feelings (Skanga)," the first dub to hit the U.K. chart, and an absolutely contagious mélange of echoed voices, ricocheting rhythms, and vast open spaces where the silence was as crucial as the sounds.

Constructed around **Johnny Clarke**'s recent hit "Everyday Wondering" (itself a thing of wonder), "Ire Feelings (Skanga)" rode the repetitious incantation of "skanga," and many European listeners, unprepared for the unbridled sound of Jamaican dub, wrote it off as a simple novelty hit. But other ears understood, as the British magazine *Street Life* acknowledged: "'Ire Feelings' helped create an unprecedented neo-commercial demand for [dub]."

Before skanga, only true fans and aficionados knew what dub sounded like. Now the whole country understood.

Not every dub was successful, no matter how legendary its creator might be. There were some frighteningly unlistenable entrants into the dub stakes, and some stultifyingly boring ones as well. But when a dub worked, there was no limit to the possibilities that it opened up. Dub versions of dubs were soon appearing, followed by dub versions of the dub version. "Ire Feelings (Skanga)," again, exists in some twenty different versions, each one radically different than the other, at the same time all remaining absolutely true to the original intentions.

Neither would advancing technology necessarily make a difference to the power of a good dub. Tubby's first efforts, many of which remain untouchable in terms of vision and earthquake, were created on an already-obsolete four-track mixer that he purchased when Dynamic Sounds Studios upgraded to eight tracks. Indeed, it might even be said that the easier it became to create a dub, the less actual ingenuity and vision was required by the maker—until we reach the 1980s and the popular face of dub was itself a faceless swamp of clever computer sounds.

Of course, there were exceptions. **Scientist** and Prince/**King Jammy** were both former students of Tubby's, learning the art as engineers at his studios before stepping out in their own right. The legendary rhythm section of Sly and Robbie, too, were deft practitioners, their approach to their own playing being so deeply rooted in dub stylings that, even after digital technology had taken over everywhere else, their own Taxi label was still pumping out "traditional" dub on single and across a stream of often-fascinating albums.

British producers Adrian Sherwood and Neil "**Mad Professor**" Fraser, too, perpetuated dub into the 1990s and beyond, with the first-named's On-U Sound empire responsible for some of the most eclectic, but simultaneously intriguing, dub sounds of all. Their strength is only amplified by Sherwood's own refusal to work within one musical genre; On-U has been home to musical styles as far apart as punk, indie rock, no-wave, and hip-hop. At the same time,

Sherwood has maintained ever-dynamic working relationships with the likes of Lee Perry, **Prince Far I**, and Dennis Alcapone.

PRINCE FAR I

A former security guard (a profession that left him scarred for life), a disc jockey and an imposing toaster, Prince Far I first recorded in 1970 under the name King Cry Cry; according to legend, another performer, **King Stitt**, was due at the studio that day, but failed to show. Rather than waste studio time, producer Coxsone Dodd allowed the erstwhile Michael James Williams, a bouncer for Studio One, to step in instead.

A couple more singles followed, but it was when Cry Cry became Far I in 1971 that things really took off. The hits "Natty Farmyard," "The Great Booga Wooga," "Musical Rocket," and "Creation Time" propelled Far I's career through the first half of the 1970s; and in 1976 he cut his first album, the booming ***Psalms for I***. But it was the following year's partnership with Joe Gibbs that truly established the Prince not only as a Jamaican superstar, but also as the voice of righteous apocalypse.

"Heavy Manners" still sounds ferocious today, three-and-a-half decades later. A damning document of the Jamaican government's recent, ruthless crackdown on violent crime (which naturally focused on nonviolent non-criminals as indiscriminately as its true targets), the single was instantly controversial, a radical roots rocker that divided Jamaica even as it catapulted Far I into infamy. And there was no holding back, either. The single was still sending shockwaves through the dance floors when Far I and Gibbs followed through with the album ***Under Heavy Manners***, a Rastafarian manifesto that not only predicted, but also paved the way for, the final fall of Babylon.

Lined up alongside Culture's ***Two Sevens Clash*** album, and Lee Perry's productions for Max Romeo and Junior Murvin, there were no more foreboding recordings to escape Jamaica. For many people truly *did* believe that Armageddon was nigh. Fulfilling a prediction that had long haunted the Rastafarian psyche, 1977 was the year when "the two sevens clashed," and Prince Far I was documenting the forthcoming apocalypse. Far I relished his reputation. Reaching back a few years, he took the rhythm track from **the Abyssinians**' Rasta devotional "Satta Massagana" and reconfigured it to host a new reading of American country singer Wink Martindale's "Deck of Cards," reloading the song's original cloying lyric with unmitigated dread and portent.

"Zion Call" followed; and with his reputation now reaching to the U.K. after he was name-checked in song by the Clash, two further albums—***Message from the King*** and ***Long Life***—pounded his vision into the popular psyche. He launched his own Cry Tuff label, and commenced a quartet of seismic dub albums, the ***Cry Tuff Dub Encounter*** series, which was responsible for some of the most scarifying dubs ever unleashed, heavy-metal essays in skull-crushing boom and bombast through which the charred remnants of melody flapped like so much post-apocalyptic flesh.

He teamed with Adrian Sherwood at On-U, linking with the Englishman's **Creation Rebel**, **Dub Syndicate**, and **Singers and Players** aggregations for a clutch of singles and two further albums, the pounding monoliths ***Dub to Africa*** and ***Prince Far I and Singers and Players***. A union with another U.K. reggae act, **the Sons of Arqa**, saw tapes of an absolutely spellbinding and utterly unrehearsed live show in late 1982 released as ***Musical Revue***, one of the greatest of all the Prince's albums.

Sadly, it was to be the last one. Prince Far I was murdered during a burglary at his home in September 1983.

Like Sherwood, the Mad Professor also works within his own absolutely unrestricted musical field, although his most satisfying projects tend to be the dub collaborations he has enacted, again, with some of the genre's most legendary practitioners—Lee Perry and Dennis Alcapone among them.

But he also successfully revitalized the careers of both U-Roy and one-time Perry protégée Susan Cadogan during the mid-1990s; and though the dub of today might never be ranked on the same mighty scale as those of the genre's earliest, bravest excursions, nevertheless we know its heritage remains in good hands.

Peter Tosh with Mick Jagger, his partner on the hot "Don't Look Back." (Photofest)

10

BEATING DOWN BABYLON: JUNIOR BYLES AND PETER TOSH

Who was the greatest reggae vocalist of all time? Bob Marley is always a good bet for that honor; Slim Smith is another contender, as are Gregory Isaacs and Dennis Brown, **Horace Andy** and Johnny Clarke.

Or **Hugh Mundell**, whose fragile, almost understated tones are just one of the elements that established his ***Africa Must Be Free by 1983*** album as one of the key discs of the late 1970s, ensuring it still sounds phenomenal today. He was just sixteen when he and producer Augustus Pablo recorded that set, and not much older when he cut the equally spellbinding ***Blackman's Foundation***. Three subsequent albums (Mundell was killed in a shooting in 1983, aged just twenty-one) could not match that opening salvo, but still that voice was *always* worth listening to.

JUNIOR BYLES

There is one other name, however, that deserves consideration just as much, if not more, than any of those others; whose own career stalled long ago, but whose records and reputation seem to grow bigger every year. Junior Byles was responsible for at least two of the songs that will be loved for as long as reggae is listened to: "Curly Locks" and "Fade Away."

He was also behind several of the most striking singles of the early 1970s, "Da Da" and "The Thanks I Get"; and, finally, he is one of that so-select handful of musicians who have worked with maverick producer Lee Perry and emerged with their own vision still intact.

Perry is one of those producers whose sonic signature is absolutely unmistakable. Byles is one of those vocalists who is just as strong.

Junior Byles was born Kerrie Byles in Kingston, Jamaica, in 1948, and was eighteen when he launched the band that would introduce him to fame in early 1967. The Versatiles were formed by Byles, Earl Dudley, and Louis Davis, and started life as just one of the countless vocal trios working the local scene at that time.

They dreamed, however, of greater things; and that summer, Byles's "The Time Has Come" came close to granting immortality when it was only narrowly beaten out at the annual Festival Song Competition. Lee Perry, then working as engineer at Joe Gibbs's studio, produced the single, together with future hits "Trust the Book" and "Worries a Yard." When Perry departed Gibbs's organization in late 1967, the Versatiles remained with Gibbs and quickly struck up a new, equally fruitful, relationship with his new chief engineer, Niney Holness. Over the next two years, the Versatiles cut a string of further 45s, including the delightfully risqué "Push It In," "Lu Lu Bell," "Long Long Time," "Pick My Pocket," and "Give It to Me."

Relations with Gibbs grew fraught, however; and, by early 1970, the Versatiles had linked again with Perry. Together, they cut a brace of fresh hits, "Children Get Ready" and "Teardrops Falling," before the Versatiles moved on...then came back again to cut their final statement, a swaggering version of Peter Tosh's "Steppin' Razor" retitled "Cutting Razor." They broke up soon after, but Byles remained with Perry; and in late 1970, the pair released a new Byles single, "What's the World Coming To?"

It was only a minor hit, but it set the scene for five years of unrelenting brilliance that included some of Perry's own best-ever productions. The militant Rastafarian anthems "Beat Down Babylon," "King of Babylon," and "Pharaoh Hiding"; the almost-hymnal "Place Called Africa"; a gorgeously atmospheric rendition of Peggy Lee's "Fever"; and the oddly suggestive "Rub Up Festival 71," a number that Byles, seemingly incredibly, considered to be an appropriate entry into the 1971 Festival Song Competition.

Even more incredibly, the judges seemed to agree with him. "Rub

Up Festival 71" actually reached the final eight selections before a radio DJ finally pointed out that the song's lyrics maybe weren't in the finest possible taste. "Rub Up Festival 71" was dropped from the finals forthwith. The following year, lesson learned, Byles entered the punch-drunk "Festival Da Da" and finished second runner-up.

"Rasta No Pickpocket," "Gwane Joshua Gwane," "Fun and Games," the wonderfully understated "When Will Better Come" ...the hits kept coming. Byles's debut album, *Beat Down Babylon*, appeared in 1973, a solid manifesto of relentless roots reggae; and then came "Curly Locks," still one of the all-time essential Jamaican 45s.

Byles and Perry parted ways soon after, the yearning "The Long Way" effectively being their final hit. But Byles still had one more masterpiece to deliver. Hot on the heels of his acclaimed second album ***Jordan***, 1975's "Fade Away" was produced by JoJo Hookim and impacted so hard in the U.K. that, five years later, it was among the first tracks recorded by producer Adrian Sherwood's New Age Steppers, coaxing a sensational vocal from ex-Slits singer Ari Up. Even today, that rendering of "Fade Away" stands as a high-water mark in the history of British reggae—as high, in fact, as the original ranks in Jamaica. "Fade Away" also made the soundtrack to the acclaimed *Rockers* movie in 1978, and earned yet another army of admirers following the film's reissue on DVD in the late 1990s.

But Byles was unraveling. Always prone to moodiness and depression, he now seemed to be losing all control of his life. Relationships, both personal and musical, first suffered and were then sundered, while the death, in August 1975, of Rastafarian figurehead Haile Selassie was the final straw. Byles attempted suicide; he was unsuccessful, but was committed to Bellevue Hospital, precipitating a retirement that effectively lasted six long years.

Sporadic attempts to maintain his career spluttered. A 1976 union with Niney Holness at least produced a savage reworking of "King of Babylon," while a handful of other singles were reasonably successful. But Byles was never in any fit state to promote or even follow through on any of them; and it would be 1982 before he resurfaced, cutting a new album for producer Blacka Morwell's Bullwackies label.

Again tragedy intervened. Byles's mother passed away; he lost his home in a fire; and his family shattered when his wife and children immigrated to America. It would be 1986 before the Wackies album, ***Rasta No Pickpocket***, was finally released, by which time Byles was living on the streets of Kingston eating garbage and unrecognized even by his friends.

He would reemerge. A handful of singles at the end of the decade put him back on the map; live work and sporadic recordings since then have kept his name alive. But compared to the majesty of the early 1970s, Byles's recording career has remained static for close to thirty years, his renown maintained more by a healthy reissue program than through his own efforts.

A brace of marvelous late 1990s compilations, the Trojan label's bonus-track-stacked *Beat Down Babylon* and Heartbeat's *Curly Locks* best-of both remain steady sellers, while a careful inspection of the wealth of rocksteady and reggae compilations currently on the market will turn up countless other gems. It is the constant rediscovery of that legacy that ensures Byles's prodigious talent remains as vital today as ever it was in the past.

PETER TOSH

Peter Tosh, too, remains vibrant, a legend whose voice was so tragically stilled (by murder) in 1987, but whose impact is still being felt today. Indeed, if Bob Marley was the melodic soul of the Wailers, the one who tempered the fury of roots with his visions of peace, Peter Tosh was the raging militant whose own vision was of a society set to rights by whatever means were necessary.

In an age where western commentators waxed eloquently of the rebel spirit that fired mid-1970s Jamaican music, Tosh was the embodiment of their assertions: a man who had no hesitation in bartering not only his celebrity but also his personal safety for the causes in which he believed—and who paid the price on so many occasions that, even today, his murder in what was officially described as a home invasion is still an object of suspicion and doubt.

Certainly Tosh never shied away from tormenting the authorities, in words and music, and in lifestyle too. His greatest recordings blaze with an indignation that, on first impression, seems no more remarkable than that exercised by so many of his contemporaries; harsh commentaries on the corruption and buck-passing that was endemic to Jamaican political life; brutal condemnations of the hypocrisy that was a second skin to so many of the country's leaders; and an evangelical drive to rid local law books of any opposition to the legalization of marijuana.

But then you listen to Tosh's performance at the One Love Peace Concert in 1978 (released on CD two decades later), to the diatribes with which he punctuated his songs, and you realize that these are not simply the words of a musician. They are the beliefs of a man for whom the words "equal rights and justice" were far more than a song lyric.

Officially, the One Love concert was billed as a commemoration of the twelfth anniversary of Haile Selassie's state visit to Jamaica in 1966. That itself was laughable. The former Ethiopian emperor was the figurehead of the Rastafarian movement, and it was their efforts who brought him to the country in the first place. To Jamaica's government, Rastafarianism was tantamount to a cultural blight whose eradication had been an unspoken policy of every leader since independence. They hijacked the significance of Selassie's visit, then, in the same way that they hijacked everything else that Jamaica strove for, and Tosh saw no value in appearing at a concert that had been stage-managed in such a fashion.

No value bar one. The stage itself.

Taking the stage immediately before the Wailers, the band he had left five years before, Tosh dressed for the occasion, wearing a black-and-white-striped karate suit and black beret. His backing band was primed for a set that would deliver Tosh's hardest-hitting songs: the premonitory "400 Years," the blade-flashing "Steppin' Razor," "Burial," "Equal Rights," "Legalise It," and the Wailers' incendiary "Get Up, Stand Up."

But nobody realized what else Tosh had in store that night; how he intended addressing himself to the 30,000 fans, journalists, cameramen, and politicians including Prime Minister Michael Manley and opposition leader Edward Seaga.

With a diatribe that ripped apart every last deception cloaking the decay that had devoured the nation's soul, with a call to arms and armed revolt. With a set that relegated the music to mere interludes between the speeches. And with the utter demolition of the concert's own title. "Peace," Tosh told the crowd, "is the diploma you get in the cemetery. On top of your grave ..."

TWENTY ESSENTIAL LIVE REGGAE ALBUMS

As the album that spawned the original hit version of "No Woman, No Cry," the song that remains Bob Marley's best-loved (and most-covered) number, the Wailers' 1975 *Live* album ignited a trend for in-concert recordings that persisted for much of the next decade, at least in western markets. More recently, the regular release of archived live recordings from the same period has done much to distill the importance of such documents—even the original "No Woman, No Cry" has been supplanted on certain Marley compilations by other live recordings.

Nevertheless, an hour or so spent in the company of a great live album is almost ... *almost* ... as good as being there; or, at least, knowing somebody who was. And here are ten of the very greatest.

Trojan Reggae Party—various artists (1971)

Recorded live in London in 1971, and the soundtrack to many a period party, *Trojan Reggae Party* preserves punchy performances from the Cimarons, **Bruce Ruffin**, **Nicky Thomas**, the Pioneers, Dandy Livingstone, Greyhound, and more. (All had scored U.K. hits recently, with Thomas's impassioned "Love of the Common People" and Ruffin's loopy "Mad About You" especially outstanding.) Hard to find, and expensive when it does turn up, but a seriously magnificent album.

Live—Burning Spear (1977)

Recorded on **Burning Spear**'s sensational visit to London in 1977, where he was accompanied by local reggae band **Aswad**, *Live* is an electrifying set that could easily be his best album ever.

Live—U-Roy (1978)

Not an album per se, *Live* was a twelve-inch EP capturing highlights of the DJ's summer 1976 visit to the U.K. Recorded at the Lyceum Ballroom, with Sly and Robbie in thunderous attendance, it whets the appetite for more. Which, sadly, has still to be delivered.

Prisoner in the Street—Third World (1980)

Third World's studio output often painted them as the soft and sweeter side of roots reggae. This set tears expectations to shreds, delivering wildfire eruptions through "96 in the Shade," "African Woman," and the title track, keeping it up so long that the vinyl has practically melted by the time you hit the end.

Live at the Music Machine—Dillinger (1981)

Recorded in London before a deliriously packed house, it is no surprise to find this album has since been repackaged as *The Best of Live.* Because that is what it is, as Dillinger travels through all his best-known numbers: "Natty Don't Need Glasses," "Roots Natty Congo," "CB 200," "Judgement Time," and, of course, "Cocaine in My Brain," a thumping celebration of white powder and its power, together with a lesson in literacy that the crowd that night knew by heart.

Live at Reggae Sunsplash—Big Youth (1983)

He opens with "I Pray Thee"/"Satta Massagana"; closes with "Hit the Road Jack"; and, in between, delivers a seething greatest-hits collection that is topped by what might be a career-best "Green Bay Killers."

Live at the Controls at Jack Ruby Sound Ocho Rios J.A. —Brigadier Jerry (1983)

A blistering dancehall celebration, with the Brigadier joined by fellow stars

Sammy Dread, Michael Prophet, and, sounding great in the midst of things, the veteran Dennis Brown.

Junjo Presents Two Big Sounds—various artists (1983)

The album that introduced the world to **Beenie Man**, a wild DJ collection that also features Dillinger, **Michael Irie**, **Fathead**, and **Ringo**, recorded live at 82 Chisholm Avenue, Kingston, in early 1983.

Prince Jammy and the Striker Lee Posse Presents Music Maker Live at the Halfway Tree Jamaica —various artists (1984)

Horace Andy, **Chaka Demus**, Don Carlos, **Super Liki**, and many more gather for a night of high-energy dancehall mania. Raw and unproduced to some ears, this album redefines excitement.

Live in Tokyo—Augustus Pablo (1991)

Pablo's reluctance to tour is good reason why there are no live recordings from his earlier period; but this set, dating from his first-ever visit to Japan in 1991, catches him making up for lost time.

Vibes Alive—Israel Vibration (1992)

Recorded in California the previous year, the long-running saga of **Israel Vibration** hits the road with the ever-seething Roots Radics.

Live On—Wailing Souls (1994)

Another album that you wish could have been recorded a decade-and-a-half before, but it wasn't, so you live with it. And that really isn't that great a hardship.

Party in Session Live—Michael Rose (1997)

Recorded at various halts on former Black Uhuru frontman's **Michael Rose**'s 1997 U.S. tour, what could have been a wearying set of revivals instead morphs into a magical celebration of past and present.

Cultural Livity—Live 1998—Culture (1998)

Spanning the years with a crowd-pleasing set, *Cultural Livity* scarcely remedies the absence of a 1970s concert recording from this most powerful of live bands, but it's still hot. Especially if you can ignore the keyboards.

Live at Reggae Sunsplash 1994—Garnett Silk (1999)

Garnett Silk was poised to become the biggest reggae star of his era when he was killed in a house fire in December 1994. Recorded at Sunsplash earlier that same year, this is thus the sound of Silk at his peak, neither beholden to the familiar versions of his greatest hits, nor particularly interested in them. If you own just one Silk album, make sure it is this one.

Live—Ziggy Marley and the Melody Makers (2000)

A handful of his father's songs could, but do not, overshadow **Ziggy Marley and the Melody Makers**' own material on an album that captures all the joy and excitement of a period Melody Makers gig.

Words of Truth—Sizzla (2000)

Two CDs for the price of one: a new studio collection and a savage **Sizzla** live set that is alone worth the price of admission.

Live—Luciano (2000)

The king of the 1990s roots-consciousness revival, **Luciano** is caught live at the end of the decade he dominated with a set that shows you how he accomplished such.

Live in Paris—Yami Bolo (2000)

Yami Bolo's version of "Curly Locks," which turns up at the end, is what clinches this as a fabulous album—but the entire performance is spot on.

Live in San Francisco—Capleton (2007)

Too many live albums are now delivered as DVDs these days, and the pros and cons of that approach are for you to decide. This stunning **Capleton** set, however, repeats the concert on an audio disc, and it's definitely worth diving into.

The following day's press united in its condemnation of Tosh's words and of the embarrassment he had heaped upon the country's leaders and upon Jamaica itself. The word "treason" was spoken, as were "insurrection" and "sedition." And when, less than five months later, Tosh was arrested for marijuana possession, then beaten almost to death by police officers, even his supporters acknowledged that he had it coming. The Peace Concert saw to that.

The *One Love Peace Concert* CD remains the ultimate Peter Tosh experience for anybody seeking to understand this most mercurial performer. But in a career that dated back to the birth of the Wailers, and took in many of the group's most crucial compositions, it is just one highlight among many. As fiery a guitarist as he was an impassioned singer-songwriter, Tosh made his greatest mark on the early band during the months when Marley was living America in 1965–1966, raising the cash for the band's future survival by working in a car plant in Delaware.

A string of new singles included Tosh's "Hoot Nanny Roll," a cover of Sir Lancelot's calypso "Shame and Scandal in the Family," "The Jerk," "Making Love," "Rasta Shook Them Up" (about Haile Selassie's visit to the island), and the rude-boy anthem "I'm the Toughest," all marking Tosh out as the group's most incisive writer. "Pound Get a Blow" and "Fire Fire," both recorded following Marley's return but with the band sliced again—this time by **Bunny Wailer**'s incarceration on a drugs charge—furthered Tosh's ambition. By the time the Wailers linked with Lee Perry at the end of the decade, a simultaneous solo career was already beckoning.

An album's worth of solo Tosh material was cut with Perry, including "(Earth's) Rightful Ruler," "400 Years," "Brand New Second Hand," "Memphis," "No Sympathy," and a reworking of the Wailers' earlier "Sinner Man," retitled "Down Presser"; other sessions with Bunny Lee and Joe Gibbs saw Tosh take further strides out on his own. "Crimson Pirate," "Ambitious Beggar," "Selassie Serenade," "The Return of Alcapone," and the truly monstrous "Maga Dog" and "Dem a fe Get a Beating" are all crucial Tosh, while "Here Comes the Judge" cast a glance back at Prince Buster's "Judge Dread" cycle by visualizing an even higher court . . . God himself . . . passing sentence upon Christopher Columbus, Francis Drake, and Vasco da Gama for crimes against Africa.

Tosh continued recording solo, but it was with his departure from the Wailers in 1973 that his career truly began striding ahead. A new version of "Brand New Second Hand" marked his first post-Wailers success; the impassioned "Legalise It" followed through, and would also title Tosh's first solo album in 1976.

Scattershot through with virulent political and religious imagery, ***Legalise It*** drew its roots from the bottom of the well, an album of relentless foreboding and drama that echoed the beliefs that shaped Tosh's lyrics. And not only his lyrics. Flip over singles like "Babylon Queendom," "Dracula," and "Legalise It" itself, and his dubs were just as uncompromising, just as iconoclastic.

His second album, ***Equal Rights***, followed seamlessly in its predecessor's footsteps, setting up that almighty confrontation at the One Love Peace Concert on April 22, 1978. And if, as some commentators claimed, he stepped back a little from direct action in the bloody aftermath of that show, he did so in remarkable company. Newly signed to the Rolling Stones' eponymous label, Tosh was opening act on the Stones' 1978 North American tour, and appeared with Mick Jagger on television's *Saturday Night Live*, performing what became Tosh's first release on the label: a revival of a Temptations song that Tosh had recorded once before with the Wailers, "(You Gotta Walk) Don't Look Back."

A hit on both sides of the Atlantic, "Don't Look Back" prefaced Tosh's next album, ***Bush Doctor***, itself an enjoyable album highlighted by sharp remakes of the oldies "I Am the Toughest" and "Them a fe Get a Beatin'." True, neither it nor its predecessors walked the same defiant walk as *Legalise It* and *Equal Rights*, but Tosh had fought his battles—and look where they got him. He received further exposure when "Steppin' Razor" was reprised for the soundtrack of the *Rockers* movie, and proved as exquisitely self-defining a choice as Jimmy Cliff's "The Harder They Come" had been for *that* movie a decade before. But the ***Mystic Man*** album was weak, and Tosh was clearly slowing.

The beating he received at the hands of the law had left him with serious health concerns, and more and more he found illness stepping in the way of his career. A new album, 1981's ***Wanted Dread or Alive***, was certainly less invigorating than those that preceded it; and while 1983's ***Mama Africa*** spawned a hit reinvention of Chuck Berry's "Johnny B. Goode," that same year also saw him play what would transpire as his last-ever major concert, at the Reggae Superjam in Kingston.

Announcing an indefinite sabbatical, broken only by the oddly-less-than-gripping in-concert ***Captured Live***, Tosh remained out of the spotlight for four long years. Then, within days of the release of what was being described as his comeback album, September 1987's ***No Nuclear War***, he was dead. And the rumors began.

From spring 1980, when the Clash hit the Poole Arts Centre. (Author's collection)

11

PUNKY REGGAE PARTY: RASTA BUSINESS IN THE U.K.

The Specials' Neville Staples hits the nail on the head. "The Clash [are] my all-time favorite band! The Clash performed with so much energy! Unlike any band I've seen then or now. I used to watch them every night when we supported them and I can't say that about any other band [except for the Specials] that I worked with, past or present, in all my years of touring."

Energetic, indeed. Of all the bands thrust into the spotlight by the first explosion of punk rock in 1976–1977, it was the Clash—alongside the Sex Pistols and the Adverts—who most firmly established the broad parameters by which the music would flourish, not to mention its political and cultural agendas.

The mid-1970s had seen British rock all but strangled by U.S. imports and Stateside sounds—even Led Zeppelin's Robert Plant screamed in an American accent. Punk set out to counter that, both sonically and lyrically. With themes ranging from the queen of England to the hookers of Soho, from the streets of London to the high-rise blocks of suburbia, English bands wanted to address English issues, and the Clash were at the top of their class.

But where they truly came into their own was with their understanding and seamless absorption of reggae.

The two musical forms were already hand in hand. The DJ at the punk mecca the Roxy Club was **Don Letts**, a Rastafarian Jamaican whose reggae record collection became the soundtrack to the Roxy, particularly during those months before the majority of punk bands had made a record. And when it came time to fuse the two together, the Clash grabbed the golden ring by recording Junior Murvin's "Police and Thieves." Frontman Joe Strummer later marveled at the sheer temerity of the band, thinking they could handle what was already established as one of the mid-1970s' premier reggae rebel yells. But he was glad they did and so are we, because it opened the door for the Clash (and, in their wake, many others) to pursue the hybrid into some astonishing corners.

The Clash's version of "Police and Thieves" was built around guitarist Mick Jones's dramatic rearrangement, with two guitars emphasizing the on- *and* offbeats. It was, as Strummer later pointed out, an utterly unique styling; any other group would've played on the offbeat alone.

Playing through the song in the studio, learning to relax within the rhythm, the Clash reinvented "Police and Thieves" for rock 'n' roll without even beginning to ruffle its own musical equilibrium, imbibing the performance with a roughness that assimilated the rebel soul of reggae at the same time as confirming the raging heart of punk. The result was a true hybrid, a garage-skank attack that not only stood head and shoulders above the rest of the material being lined up for the Clash's debut album, it dwarfed almost anything being done in the name of punk at that time.

And that despite "Police and Thieves" almost not making it onto the album. The band themselves never considered it to be anything more than a fun warm-up before the serious business of recording their own songs got underway; but when thirteen Clash originals still clocked in at less than twenty-nine minutes, it became clear that they had to add something to the album. Given the choice between a song they all enjoyed playing or the handful of other band compositions that had already been put aside, there was no competition.

Neither were the six minutes given over to the song to be the Clash's only nod toward reggae; if that had been the case, the entire performance might well have ended up reeking of tokenism or worse ... Johnny Rotten, after all, had only recently complained that white bands trying to play reggae was a form of cultural exploitation.

Throughout their repertoire, the band—Jones in particular—experimented with sounds and ideas they'd picked up from the Jamaican records that Simonon and Strummer were stockpiling: dropouts, phasing, so many little snatches that may not even have been noticeable individually. Together, however, they conjured up the picture of a very English record, cut through with very Kingston stylings. Then, when it came time to recruit a producer for a new single, "Complete Control," they turned not to one of the expected giants of the British studio scene, but to Lee "Scratch" Perry.

"Complete Control" promptly gave the band their first Top 30 hit, reaching #28; it would be followed by "Clash City Rockers," an inspired effort that simultaneously ushered in what amounted to the Clash's own golden age of rock 'n' roll: "(White Man) In Hammersmith Palais," "Tommy Gun," "English Civil War," and a ferocious version of Bobby Fuller's "I Fought the Law," all either feeding into, or drawing their inspiration out of, the Clash's fascination with reggae—both the music and the outlaw culture.

That their liaison with Lee Perry contrarily produced a decidedly rock-oriented song only increases the admiration with which one must regard this particular sequence. Perry's original mix was indeed rooted in reggae and dub techniques, and many other bands would have stuck with that, whatever the end result sounded like. The Clash, however, realized when something just didn't feel right; and the moment Perry was gone, Mick Jones remixed the song completely, subverting the rhythm, raising the guitars, and completely restructuring the piece. Even more radically, a version of the Maytals' "Pressure Drop" (a live favorite through the Clash's spring, 1977 White Riot tour) recorded at the same session was scrapped altogether.

There were no hard feelings; indeed, the Clash's refusal to stick with his original vision only impressed Perry further. Hooking up with Bob Marley later in London, Perry talked glowingly of the Clash and enthusiastically about the punk scene that was absorbing the lessons of roots reggae into a musical stew of its own creation. Marley responded by writing "Punky Reggae Party," a song that would itself become a virtual national anthem for punk.

Other songs in this sequence of sudden Clash gems stand out. "Jail Guitar Doors" was a song Strummer had been playing with his last band; recorded for a B-side, it now boasted a new verse by Jones furthering the Clash's outlaw status by aligning the band with sundry past musical rebels, including Toots Hibbert of the Maytals. That band's "54-46, That's My Number," written about Hibbert's time in jail for marijuana possession, was also name-checked in the new lyric. Another Jamaican rude-boy anthem, **the Slickers**' "Johnny Too Bad," was mentioned in "The Prisoner." But it was with "(White Man) In Hammersmith Palais" that the Clash truly cemented their legend.

Musically the song is peerless, following through on the threat of "Police and Thieves" with a tight rocker rhythm spat out through seething guitars. But it was lyrically that "(White Man)" came into its own. In essence, it was based on Strummer's experiences at a Dillinger show at the West London venue of the same name, standing through the support acts (**Leroy Smart** and Delroy Wilson) and watching as an apparently unified black-and-white audience nevertheless divided down stereotypical cultural lines—and then comparing this dichotomy to the punk movement's own ongoing dissolution into countless factional squabbles.

The entire Clash catalogue (with the Jones-less exception of *Cut the Crap*, their final album) is recommended to absolutely anyone who has never heard it. But some moments are recommended more than others, beginning with another reggae cover, **Willi Williams**'s "Armagideon Time."

The song was originally brought into the band's repertoire as a soundcheck warm-up, then promoted to an incendiary encore. In both instances, the Clash stripped it back to its bass-driven basics, from which they developed a driving jam, Strummer snarling the lyric over one of Simonon, Jones, and Headon's most unified performances yet. Even more powerfully, they then extended the original song into genuine dub territory, emerging with a ten-minute epic that would as thoroughly redirect rock reggae as "Police and Thieves" had reinvented it two years earlier. Indeed, in the annals of punk-and-after's manifold experiments with such a fusion, only **the Ruts**' "Jah War" even came close to equaling the Clash's accomplishment. Everyone else was left at the starting gate, although the Clash would not be alone for long.

IN A RUT

Politically aware, but rarely sloganeering, the Ruts stood at the crossroads of punk, reggae, and that peculiar brand of skinhead chanting that the media termed Oi! They gave their heart to all three. The fact that they accomplished it all with just one official album, and a handful of singles, only emphasizes their power. If the Ruts had survived into the 1980s, the 1980s as we know them would probably never have happened.

The band members were West London schoolfriends whose most regular gig was their local pub; they were just another provincial band, with provincial gigs in provincial bars. But they also played benefits for Rock Against Racism, a cause that quickly introduced them to **Misty in Roots**, an excellent reggae band from the same neighborhood as the Ruts. It was an inspired coupling that not only honed the two bands' musical abilities, it also sharpened their appreciation of one another's work. Other white English bands had dipped into the reggae songbook, to varying degrees of success; the Ruts were the first (the Clash notwithstanding) to make that songbook their own. But by the end of 1978, the Ruts' hybrid glory was ready to go.

"In a Rut," their first single, offered little indication of the band's musical strength. A fairly straightforward punk anthem, it was released on Misty in Roots's own People Unite label, and lined the band up as just another punk group. Their live show, however, spoke otherwise; and in early 1979, the Ruts released their first undisputed classic and signature song, "Babylon's Burning." (It had originally been called "London's Burning," but the Clash had been there already.)

Bassist Vince Seggs recalled how vocalist Malcolm Owen "really got into the ska look: the hats and clothes. It was a real crossover point: Malcolm, in his inimitable way, started to wear a porkpie hat and a mauve two-tone suit. It was a bit of a fashion thing but it was kinda normal really, because I came out of ska and Motown; that's what I listened to as a kid.

And with cross-fertilization and all that, blah blah, gigs with Misty in Roots, all the reggae bands in London, it was kind of normal that 2-Tone would come out of that. And as the 2-Tone thing picked up, we were getting some of that crowd to come along to see us."

The Ruts would even be recruited to back a genuine ska hero, Laurel Aitken, on his "comeback" single, "Rudi Got Married." Even so, Virgin, who signed the Ruts in the spring of 1979, were as surprised as anyone when the band sealed the deal with a hit. "Babylon's Burning" rammed the Ruts into the Top 10; "Something That I Said" kept the band in the Top 30; and in October, the Ruts released their debut album, *The Crack*.

What an album that was, from the police siren that opens side one wailing into "Babylon's Burning" through to the closing "Jah War," the culmination of the Ruts' dub-punk hybrid. Written following race riots that shook the predominantly black Southall neighborhood, and saw 300-plus arrests, the militant "Jah War" was promptly slapped with an unspoken broadcast ban. But it confirmed the Ruts' ascendancy all the same. When "Staring at the Rude Boys" brought them another hit, the Ruts had the world at their feet. Their second album beckoned, and so did America.

But behind the scenes, all was not well. Malcolm Owen was nursing a serious drug habit, and though he tried to clean up following a string of cancelled gigs, he then celebrated his sobriety by getting high once again. He died from a massive overdose on July 14, 1980.

The Specials, undisputed heads of the so-called 2-Tone ska revival, had landed their first major break opening for the Clash the previous year. Unashamedly, they drew their musical inspiration from many of the same sources (and scratchy old Trojan label albums). And unapologetically, they threw themselves toward notions that the Clash had hitherto owned exclusive rights to: writing new rock songs around old ska rhythms; updating classics and making them their own; and, most of all, painting a picture of a society that had firmly, it seemed, embraced its own self-destruction—1979 also saw Margaret Thatcher come to power.

Now, while she invoked the specters of the draft and restricted immigration as short, sharp cures for the evils of unemployment, the Specials joined the Clash as the loudest (commercially viable) voices raised against her. The 2-Tone group had already published their manifesto in the form of a devastating debut album; the Clash, recognizing much of their own blueprint in those same grooves, were now duty-bound to respond in kind.

That same year's ***London Calling*** double album was only the first volley. The next twelve months of the Clash's career were to be devoted to an unparalleled spree of musical insurrection.

Two successive singles, the chattering "Bankrobber" and the brittle skank "The Call Up," kept the band buoyant through much of 1981. A U.K. tour with Jamaican DJ **Mikey Dread** (who also produced "Bankrobber") saw the Clash literally sparking with livewire energy; and their latest U.S. tour saw *Rolling Stone*, of all graying institutions, welcoming them with one of the most honest appraisals they'd received in three years, a front cover headlined "Rebels with a cause and a hit album."

The Clash's next album, ***Sandinista!***, was an almost impertinent triple-disc set—so much material were they accumulating—while the ***Black Market Clash*** compilation of rarities and outtakes remains an object lesson in everything that made the band magical. According to the band, the collection was only ever intended as a stopgap release between the Clash's third and fourth albums; yet in both its original ten-inch vinyl form and its expanded ***Super Black Market Clash*** CD incarnation, this collection of non-album odds and sods proved to be the most startling document yet of the Clash's development.

Chronologically, it spanned the three years that took the Clash from the skewed punk overdrive of "Cheat" and "Capital Radio" through "The Prisoner," "City of the Dead," and "Pressure Drop" B-sides and onto the towering peaks of "Armagideon Time," "Bankrobber," and its own dub flipside, "Robber Dub." Conceptually, however, it also revealed the group as the smartest white dance band around—a point hammered home, ironically or otherwise, by the exhumation of "Time Is Tight," a "Hammersmith Palais"–era outtake that buzzed with excitement, energy, and its own almost-palpable conviction that for the first time in music history, a bunch of English kids were beating the hallowed gods of Stax at their own game.

Well, they'd already taken on Studio One and Treasure Isle.

Sean Paul at the 2006 American Music Awards. (ABC/Photofest)

12

IF YOU LIKE *EXODUS*, YOU'LL LOVE THIS: COVERING THE WAILERS' GREATEST LP

***Exodus* was Bob Marley and the Wailers' mightiest triumph.** Recorded in London in early 1977, with Marley still recovering from an assassination attempt back in Jamaica the previous year, it was rooted in his native land's own recent embrace of roots; indeed, Marley went into the sessions contemplating recording a full-on dub set, which would have been only his second ever.

That idea (sadly) never came to fruition, but *Exodus* would still emerge a darker, heavier, angrier generation than its predecessors had ever been. Its mood had been stamped by records like Culture's *Two Sevens Clash* and Peter Tosh's *Legalise It*, and informed by the enraged consciousness of Prince Far I and Tappa Zukie, each of whom released heavy roots material that warned of both an Armageddon to come (and one that was already unfolding).

In Jamaica, *Exodus* ruled the airwaves for much of the rest of the year. In Britain, it spawned three hit singles during 1977 alone (and a fourth in 1980), breaking the band into the Top 10 album chart for the first time; in the U.S., it readily consolidated the breakthrough success of *Rastaman Vibration*. *Exodus* was the peak of the Wailers' development, the masterpiece they had been threatening for so long, and it was instantly proclaimed as such. When *Kaya* was released the following year, even the knowledge that it had been conceived in tandem with its predecessor did not prevent fans and critics alike from hammering it.

It might be overly ambitious to agree with *Time* magazine's assertion that *Exodus* was the greatest album of the twentieth century. But it is certainly among the most important.

So let's see what other performers have made of its contents ...

"NATURAL MYSTIC"

Horace Andy's spectral dance through "Natural Mystic" opens his *Wicked Dem a Burn* album, itself a collection of his pioneering mid-1970s work with producer Bunny Lee.

"SO MUCH THINGS TO SAY"

Bunny Wailer, of course, was a founding member of the Wailers, alongside Bob Marley and Peter Tosh, and "So Much Things to Say" was cut as part of a tribute album, ***Hall of Fame***, released in 1995 to mark what would have been Marley's fiftieth birthday. A sassier vocal than Marley ever fashioned floats over an arrangement that itself might have stepped out of the Wailers' days as a vocal trio nods to their roots, then, at the same time it acknowledges the changes that Marley had been through since then.

A friend of Marley since he was seven, Bunny Wailer was never the most prolific songwriter in the Wailers, although when he did put pen to paper it was with devastating results. Only after he quit the group in 1973, a few months ahead of Peter Tosh's departure, did he reveal himself to have been writing all along, but concentrating on a spiritual angle that the Wailers themselves could never have accommodated. His final numbers with the band, on the *Burnin'* album, were "Hallelujah Time" and "Pass It On," and these became the template around which his solo career would take shape.

Early solo singles "Searching for Love," "Trod On," "Lifeline," and "Arabs Oil Weapon" led up to the 1976 release of his first album, ***Blackheart Man***. ***Protest***, ***Struggle***, and ***In Father's House*** followed, but made little impression compared to the activities of his erstwhile bandmates. But Marley's death in May 1981 ignited a new enthusiasm in Wailer. Teaming with the Roots Radics, the studio band led by Sly and Robbie, Wailer dipped back into the old band's Studio One catalogue to record two albums' worth of material by way of tribute to his fallen comrade: ***Bunny Wailer Sings the Wailers*** and ***Tribute***.

He returned to touring, too, for the first time since his last days with the Wailers (the *Live* album caught his opening shows); and the late 1980s saw Wailer embark upon his most prolific spell in a decade with a string of albums divided between the expected rootsy concerns and an emphatic dancehall vibe. Today he appears more concerned with politics, and enjoying his status as an elder spokesman of reggae, than competing in the musical marketplace—but Wailer's immortality was confirmed long ago.

"GUILTINESS"

Confirming reggae's advance into, and absorption by, the American mainstream, "Guiltiness" was one of a dozen Marley/Wailers songs subjected to what could have been (but thankfully wasn't) that most ignominious of fates, the superstar-duet album. ***Chant Down Babylon*** featured the likes of Lauryn Hill, Erykah Badu, **Busta Rhymes**, Aerosmith, and MC Lyte adding their vocals and imaginings to Marley's original recordings. "Guiltiness" paired the *Exodus* original with Mr. Cheeks and the Lost Boyz—a late-1990s rap act whose interjections and interruptions actually lend much fresh atmosphere to the performance.

"THE HEATHEN"

Jamaican saxophonist **Dean Fraser** grasped "The Heathen" for his 1994 instrumental album *Dean Plays Bob*, a somewhat more jazz-lite collection than Fraser's traditionally energetic playing might have led one to expect, but an enjoyable romp regardless.

"EXODUS"

Of all the re-creations that *Exodus*, both the album as a whole and its individual contents, have been subjected to, none can match *Ten Commandments*, the 1978 album that saw toaster I-Roy take nine of the ten cuts that comprised the original *Exodus* album and—having rerecorded the backing tracks with the roots band **Chalawa**—re-imagine them as indeed the Ten Commandments. (Chalawa's unadorned dub was itself released as, sensibly, ***Exodus Dub***.)

Wholly apocalyptic, electrifyingly assaultive, even true believers will confess that, at its best, *Ten Commandments* is superior to the original album at least in terms of an all-pervading mood of danger and foreboding. Certainly "Commandment Four," voiced over a slow-burning "Exodus"; "Commandment Six" ("Natural Mystic") and "Commandment Seven" ("Jamming") are unimpeachable, while the one non-album track that makes it aboard, "Put It On" (replacing "Turn Your Lights Down Low") is as dynamically self-aggrandizing a performance as I-Roy has ever voiced.

An outspoken but often humorous performer who took his stage name as a tribute to U-Roy, I-Roy was one of the superstar toasters who made the 1970s such challenging fun. "Musical Pleasure" was his first hit; and through the early part of the decade, he recorded with most every major producer in Kingston, building up several compilation albums' worth of seething, primal successes: "Hot Bomb," "Make Love," "Rose of Sharon," "Mood for Love," "Melinda," "Problems in Life," "Musical Drum Sound," "Sound Education," "Rasta on a Sunday," "Sidewalk Killer," "Magnificent Seven," and "High Jacking." Indeed, by the time I-Roy's debut album, *Presenting*, was released in 1973, it already doubled as a greatest-hits collection.

That pattern remained true for subsequent albums, as I-Roy matched his musical and lyrical prowess with a keen eye for technology and sound, working as house producer at Channel One studios and overseeing such seminal roots efforts as John Holt's "Up Park Camp," **the Meditations**' "Woman Is Like a Shadow," and more.

His own recordings took a backseat during this period but by 1975 he was back on track, enjoying such hits as "The Black Bullet," "I Man Time," "Welding," "Forward Yah!," and "Roots Man," while also inaugurating a hilarious vinyl war with rival DJ Prince Jazzbo. The pair duked it out on wax for some months, while I-Roy continued his own path with the gems "Natty Down Deh," "Ital Dish," "Musical Air Raid," and a remarkable reinvention of John Holt's "A Quiet Place" (AKA "Man Next Door"), suitably restructured as "A Noisy Place." In the space of just eight months, I-Roy placed thirteen hits on the Jamaican charts.

Wildly prolific, I-Roy continued releasing albums, with *Ten Commandments* just one jewel among many; his late '70s output for the Virgin Frontline label is singularly brilliant. But health problems caused him to slow down; financial difficulties worsened his position; and, at one point, one of Jamaica's most legendary toasters was reportedly living rough, his only assistance coming from his mentally challenged son. In 1999, the great I-Roy passed away from heart problems at the Spanish Town hospital.

"JAMMING"

The best-known footage of Bob Marley performing "Jamming" finds him with eyes tightly shut for much of the song, as though he is trying to forget an alternate version with very rude words. It is one of life's crueler tricks that many listeners might expect this to be that version.

It is very easy to regard **Pato Banton** as a novelty performer, an understandable assumption based on the evidence of his earliest hits and best-known material, but an unfair one regardless. Certainly he came to fame with the hit "Hello Tosh, Got a Toshiba"; certainly too, his "Do Not Sniff the Coke" remains one of the most humorous exaltations of marijuana ever released. But Banton's overall repertoire is good-natured rather than comical; and if the impersonations of his mother that slip into his lyrics can still crack a smile, his intentions remain honorable. His ***Never Give In*** debut album, from 1987, rates highly whatever your reggae criteria might be, with adroit handling of both lightweight social and heavier cultural issues, while his occasional partnerships with the Beat's **Ranking Roger** have also unleashed some remarkable music.

His version of "Jamming," found on an admittedly rather grueling compilation called *Covers for Lovers*, epitomizes the Banton approach—as breezy as the best summer day, as light as the sweetest beachfront cocktail. Some sour-faced Marley analysts might well say it completely misses the point of the original song. But it also sticks to the lyric and does so with joy; and if there is a rude version somewhere out there, we continue to be spared from hearing it.

"WAITING IN VAIN"

One of that select handful of Marley/Wailers songs that has not only been translated into the rock idiom, but might even have benefitted from the journey, "Waiting in Vain" was delightfully covered by singer Annie Lennox on her 1995 all-covers collection *Medusa*. Stripped of all but the specter of its Caribbean heritage, "Waiting in Vain" emerges instead as a lush ballad, with Lennox's full vocal holding back on its traditional foghorn tendencies to wrap as sensitively around the lyric as the lyric has always embraced the melody.

"TURN YOUR LIGHTS DOWN LOW"

Another case of Marley's original colliding with the best intentions of a latter-day artist, former Fugee Lauryn Hill's studio-crafted duet with Marley appeared on *Chant Down Babylon* (see above) but might be better known for its service on the soundtrack to the movie *The Best Man*. Which is an inauspicious place to find such a sensitive reading, but there you go.

"THREE LITTLE BIRDS"

Another soundtrack, another day. But if you have ever wondered what Bob Marley's son Ziggy would sound like wrapping one of his father's most gleeful lyrics around toaster **Sean Paul**'s fevered interjections, the computer-animated comedy *Shark Tale* should be your first destination.

David "Ziggy" Marley was the first of three children born to Bob and Rita Marley, and the eldest son among the eleven children his father eventually sired. A full accounting of Marley's biological children reads like this: Imani, his eldest, was born to Cheryl Murray in 1963, and the next three were his children with Rita—Cedella (1967), David (1968), and Stephen (1972). The remainder were born of his various mistresses: Robert (1972), Rohan (1972), Karen (1973), Julian (1975), Ky-Mani (1976), Damian (1978), and Madeka (1981). Bob also adopted two children, Rita's daughters Sharon and Stephanie.

Often appearing onstage as an exuberant child dancer during the last years of Marley's life, he and siblings Stephen, Cedella, and Sharon then made their vinyl debut with the single "Children Playing in the Streets," a Marley composition that was credited to the Melody Makers. Royalties from the single, incidentally, were gifted to the United Nations' International Year of the Child.

There was no doubt that the Melody Makers would eventually launch a career in earnest. The question was, *when?* Ziggy and Stephen performed at Bob's funeral, re-creating their father's dance moves during a short set by the **I-Threes** and the surviving Wailers; the Melody Makers also performed a short set of his best-known songs at a concert marking what would have been Marley's thirty-seventh birthday.

Ultimately, however, it would be 1984 before the quartet truly stepped out in its own right, releasing their debut album ***Play the Game Right*** in 1985. ***Hey World!*** (1986) and ***Conscious Party*** (1988) followed; and the Melody Makers launched into a period of mainstream success, with two successive albums, *Conscious Party* and 1989's ***One Bright Day***, earning the group two successive Best Reggae Album Grammys. Only the preeminence of Shabba Ranks's ***As Raw as Ever*** deprived them of a third, for 1991's ***Jahmekya***.

One can argue endlessly over whether Ziggy in particular, or any of his other singing siblings, can truly be described as the musical heir to their father. For some listeners, blood speaks louder than the occasional dodgy song; for others, the second-generation Marleys received no more of a head start in the creative stakes than the offspring of any other musical superstar, from Jakob Dylan to Julian Lennon.

But recent albums by Ziggy Marley (2011's ***Wild and Free***), Stephen (the intrigue-laden roots explorations of ***Revelation Part One***), and Damian (the hip-hop-infused *Welcome to Jam Rock*) all prove that the apple did not fall too far from the tree. Which is more than can be said for some of the other famous names out there.

"ONE LOVE"/"PEOPLE GET READY"

Sam Bush's New Grass Revival was a bluegrass band featuring demon picker Bela Fleck. In 1984, they included the closing medley from the *Exodus* album on their own first disc in a couple of years, *On the Boulevard*. And how did the original fusion of the Wailers and the Impressions get along with the frantic sounds of wild Appalachia? A lot better than you might expect!

Ari Up—New Age Stepper, Slit, and superstar. (Georgia Kral)

13

IN THE BEGINNING, THERE WAS ARI: THE EARTHBEAT OF THE SLITS

Compile a list of the greatest reggae records ever cut by non-Jamaican artists, and chances are that Ari Up will feature on at least a couple of them. A deeply dubbed rendition of "I Heard It Through the Grapevine" that was almost wasted as a B-side to **the Slits**' first single (it should have been an A-side in its own right); a scarifying version of John Holt's "Man Next Door," recorded toward the end of that same band's career; "The Scheisse Song," agitating on her final recording, with producer Adrian Sherwood's New Age Steppers; and a gorgeous rendition of Junior Byles's "Fade Away," her first recording with that same band. All are highlights not only of Up's catalogue, but of the field in general.

The Slits' ***Cut*** album, meanwhile, remains the acid test for anybody who reckons white reggae has added nothing more than commercial oatmeal to the original genre; while Up's solo ***Dread More Dan Dead*** album, in 2005, upped the ante even further, emerging both the most courageous, and possibly contentious, contribution to the canon since Eric Clapton first took "I Shot the Sheriff" and transformed it into a sound that even bleach-blond, screechy-voiced English schoolteachers could love.

The erstwhile Ariane Forster (John Lydon is her stepfather) formed the Slits in January 1977, helming an all-girl punk band at a time when female rockers were still expected to be the girl next door. Scarcely able to play their instruments, and getting by on sheer determination and attitude, the Slits were touring with the Clash within weeks of their formation, and still finding their way for some months thereafter. Veteran rock critics, and many punk fans too, loathed them; even in a musical genre that prided itself on its participants' lack of virtuosity, the Slits' ability to leap the thin line that divides amateurism from incompetence was too much for many to bear.

The American magazine *Rolling Stone* caught the Slits live in London in August 1977, and insisted that "any current American audience would reward [them] with a shower of bottles"; the *New Musical Express* described their earliest shows as "shambolic and puerile." But that same publication also detected the "hint of something special [that] make[s] these silly displays so frustrating," and the band confirmed that observation when they recorded their first session for BBC Radio's John Peel at the end of September. Primitive still, and oft-times infuriating, the session nevertheless breathed fire and fury, and might well have been the most exciting sound to air on the radio all year. Peel certainly thought so; he replayed the session four times over the next three months.

The Slits were gathering supporters and admirers. By the time the band inked a record deal in 1979 (with original drummer Palmolive replaced by future Siouxsie and the Banshees percussionist Budgie), all of those early condemnations had been forgotten.

In the studio with **Dennis Bovell**, one of the homegrown heroes of Britain's own reggae scene, the Slits recorded *Cut*, an album that defied both the band's limitations and the media's skepticism. Contagious, courageous, and even commercial without a hint of compromise, it layered broad swaths of dub intent across brash punk immediacy, brittle and brutal in equal proportions.

"The [Slits'] aspirations were so massive," Budgie recalls. "When we went in to do *Cut*, the brief to Dennis [Bovell], if there was one, was a cross between *Saturday Night Fever* and *Spirits Having Flown*, the Bee Gees album. It's got to be dance, it's got to have reggae ... this is a tall order, you know? But it was totally crazed, and it worked. The next thing I remember which caught me like that was the first Public Image album, where you went, 'Whoops, what's this sound? What's all this about?'"

THE PUBLIC IMAGE

The Clash, the Slits, and the Ruts were not the only punk bands to look toward reggae. From Belfast, Stiff Little Fingers cut a stunning cover of the Wailers' "Johnny Was"; Elvis Costello blended dark reggae rhythms into his 1977 hit "Watching the Detectives"; and the Adverts' **T. V. Smith** commented upon Britain's growing social dislocation with the biting "Wheels Out of Gear," capturing the sheer hopelessness of early 1980s youth better than anyone save the Specials. The comedy troupe Albertos y Lost Trios Paranoias even got in on the fun with the remarkable "Snuffing in a Babylon," a song that rounded up so many rootsy preoccupations that it is amazing it lasted less than two minutes.

Billy Idol's Generation X outraged their record company with their request to release a dub version of their debut album (they were refused permission), while Roogalator, a band led by American funk aficionado Danny Adler, went even further. "We were the only white band at that time to play live dub reggae," Adler boasts. They did so nightly; as the quartet segued from "Tasty Two" into "Humanitation," the PA would leap into the fray as the band's soundman unleashed his own stash of backward tapes, surreal grooves, and wild echo and panning, while Adler, eschewing his regular vocals for unrestrained toasting, let rip on the guitar effects.

And at the top of the pile, Sex Pistol John Lydon *né* Rotten followed up a longstanding love of dub and reggae by advising Virgin Records on the creation of their Frontline reggae label. He joined company chief Richard Branson in Kingston to line up the label's first signings; and then, back in the U.K., formed Public Image Ltd., a band whose grasp of dub techniques and rhythms shattered glass across two utterly seminal albums. Both their eponymous debut and the sophomore ***Metal Box*** offered an inescapable blast of chilled machinery, crying screeches, and dense metal dub loops, with the latter still glowering as one of the most revolutionary records ever made. Or marketed.

Originally released as three twelve-inch singles tightly packaged in a metal tin, *Metal Box* is utterly uncompromising, exorcizing the ghosts of Lydon's punk past (or even the first album's melodic sensibilities) in favor of a subterranean rumble over which vocals toast, chant, and yowl with disorienting disdain. Yet it spawned a hit single, the "Death Disco" remix of the album's "Swan Lake," and *Metal Box* remains one of the defining moments in rock's relationship with the outer limits of reggae: "Eerie, futuristic art punk," as *Rolling Stone* put it, "with dub bass and slashing guitar."

Public Image never followed up on *Metal Box*, but how could they be expected to? Only Can, the early 1970s German band whose own fascination with rhythm and effect had long since established them as a Lydon favorite, had even glanced down the cul-de-sacs that *Metal Box* so triumphantly torched, and Public Image too knew there was no going further. The transitional *Flowers of Romance* album was their ticket back to something approaching mainstream sonics; and the remainder of their career (both in its original form and via a late-2000s reunion) saw them remaining in that same general ballpark. *Metal Box* itself remains unrepeatable, unassailable, and utterly unrepentant.

While the joyously frenetic "Typical Girls" toyed with the U.K. chart, and its B-side, "I Heard It Through the Grapevine," hypnotized the clubs, *Cut* echoed and scratched through ten triumphant tracks that told the musical story of the Slits-so-far as shattered through a prism of rhythm. "New Town," with its deep, clattered echo; "Love and Romance," turned turtle across Bovell's dub remix "Liebe and Romanze"; the swaggering "Ping Pong Affair"; "Shoplifting," with its triumphant cry of "Do a runner!"—*Cut* is bratty, beastly, and often belligerent. But it is also a work of staggering beauty.

A tour followed with veteran trumpet player Don Cherry made an honorary Slit (his daughter, Neneh, also appeared as backing vocalist); but the band quit Island soon after, resurfacing in March 1980 with a triptych of remarkable 45s on the Rough Trade label.

The deeply tribal "In the Beginning, There Was Rhythm" was an invocation of the spiritual energies of Jamaican *nyahbinghi* even as it crashed into wholly uncharted territories. A second single,

"Man Next Door," followed, being a solid revision of the Holt song that paved the way for every cover the song has endured since then. And the haunting "Animal Space" completed this trilogy of singles, while Up alone took time away from the band to lead Adrian Sherwood's newly formed New Age Steppers to further glory. Their take on "Fade Away," even more than the excellent album that followed, epitomized not only Up's love of reggae music, but also her instinctual understanding of it.

The Slits reconvened with a sensibly titled second album, ***The Return of the Giant Slits***, a still-staggering accomplishment that found the band resolutely dedicated to exploring the furthest periphery of the reggae-punk experiment. "Earthbeat" was the haunting opener, all insistent percussion and Up's keening chant wrapped to a traumatic toast while the drums sought out a contradictory rhythm. It was savagely beautiful, the first putatively rock-related release to investigate such stylings—but the album sank and the Slits followed, breaking up within weeks of their next U.K. tour. It would be a quarter of a century before they returned.

They were remembered with their final session for DJ John Peel, featuring lengthy throbs through "In the Beginning, There Was Rhythm"; the album's "Difficult Fun"; and finally "Earthbeat," a mantric pulse over which Up's most tender vocal cajoled and seduced with a guile that surprised even the band's fans. It was not a fluke. While her bandmates retired from the music industry, Up threw herself back into the New Age Steppers in time for the collective's second album, summer, 1982's ***Action Battlefield***; it was followed the next year by ***Foundation Steppers***.

Like the Steppers' first LP, both are divided between wild experimentation and powerful melody; like much of Sherwood's work from this period, the sense of adventure is often placed in greater focus than the listener's comfort. But occasionally everything slams into place ("Observe Life" is especially magnificent), and when it does, all three albums are indispensable.

Slowly, though, Up drifted away, only surfacing occasionally for guest appearances here and there. Catch her if you can on

Terranova's *Hitchhiking Nonstop with No Particular Destination* and *Peace Is Tough* albums, or the *Village Voice*–compiled *Wish You Were Here*, a benefit record for victims of the Twin Towers attack. There she transformed the Cookies' "Don't Say Nothing Bad About My Baby" into "Don't Say Nothing Bad About NY," about her newly adopted home (after years spent living in Jamaica).

2005 saw her full-blown return to action with *Dread More Dan Dead*, a jittery, juddering brew that captured her love for contemporary Jamaican sounds while remaining informed by her grounding in their past. The Slits, too, returned, first for a tentative EP, 2006's ***Revenge of the Killer Slits***, and then for a full-blown album, ***Trapped Animal***.

In truth, anybody expecting some kind of updated collision of the auteur punk of *Cut* and the world-music miasma of *Return of the Giant Slits* was in for a shock. *Trapped Animal*'s closest relative, at least across the first couple of songs, was an extra-sassy **Lily Allen**—who herself had broken through with a wonderfully breezy and super-sassy take on the reggae music that her dad's friend Joe Strummer used to play her when she was a child. (Dad, by the way, is British comedian Keith Allen.)

At the same time, however, "Pay Rent" was one of several tracks that looked directly back to *Cut*'s cult of assertive dub-punk, while the frantic "Rejects" was one of a handful more that could have stepped out of the even-earlier incarnation of the band that is preserved on their first two John Peel sessions.

Somewhat reluctantly, it should be acknowledged that *Trapped Animal* only rarely tapped the heights reached by *Dread More Dan Dead*; that the accompanying horn section sounded like it would have been far happier at a 2-Tone revival party; and that if you don't like the aforementioned Lily Allen, the real trapped animal in the room when the album plays will be you. But Up retained and remained one of the most distinctive voices in rock, and nobody could write songs and rhythms like the Slits.

Trapped Animal would be the reunited Slits' sole release. She collaborated with Lee Perry, X. A. Cute, and Dubblestandart, but Up was ill, undergoing treatment for the cancer that would kill her in 2010. A single, "Hello, Hell Is Very Low," recorded with Perry in 2010, was the final release of her lifetime.

There would be one final album, however, a reunion with Adrian Sherwood and the New Age Steppers for ***Love Forever*** (released in 2012), and a savage reassertion of all that was once so breathlessly astonishing about Up, her attitude, and her approach. Defiant, dramatic, and driving, "Bad for My Nerves" is laugh-aloud freneticism; "The Fury of Ari" is dense and haunted; and "Musical Terrorist" could as easily be autobiography as it is a statement of past and future intent. There will be no more music from Ari Up, but what we have speaks to everyone.

The greatest reggae story ever told: Perry Henzell's *The Harder They Come*.
(Author's collection)

14

SKANKING ON THE BIG SCREEN: REGGAE ON FILM

If you're looking for a crash course in Jamaican musical history, but don't want to turn your television off, there are a wealth of documentary features that could keep you glued to the armchair from now until Christmas.

Horace Ove's movie of the 1969 reggae festival at Wembley in London, the simply titled ***Reggae*** (1970), is raw and enthusiastic, a chance to see Desmond Dekker, the Maytals, the Pyramids, and more in action years before the movie cameras ventured into a Jamaican concert hall. Or, for later tastes, James P. Lewis's film of the 1978 One Love Peace Concert, ***Heartland Reggae*** (1980), catches Marley and the Wailers, Peter Tosh, Inner Circle, and more in career-peaking form, and leads off a lengthy shelf-full of subsequent reggae-concert movies.

Alan Greenberg's ***Land of Look Behind*** (1982), Oliver Hill's ***Coping with Babylon*** (2007), and Helene Lee's ***The First Rasta*** (2009) head off the heap of pertinent examinations of life and faith on the island.

Wolfgang Büld's ***Reggae in a Babylon*** looks at the growth of sound systems and reggae in the U.K. in the late 1970s; the 2-Tone team's ***Dance Craze*** does the same for the ska revival of the early 1980s; and Moon Ska's ***Bang*** captures a similar moment in the U.S. almost two decades later.

But what if you want to escape reality for a couple of hours, and enjoy reggae music in the same way that Beatles fans thrill to *Help!*, or glam lovers groove to *Velvet Goldmine*?

The pickings are certainly slimmer. But compared to the mountain of trash that has been thrown at rock 'n' rolling movie buffs over the years, if you like Bob Marley, there are a few movies that you *have* to see.

THE HARDER THEY COME (1973)

Starring: Jimmy Cliff, Janet Bartley, Carl Bradshaw, Ras Daniel Hartman, Basil Keane, Robert Charlton, Winston Stona
Produced and directed by Perry Henzell; written by Perry Henzell and Trevor D. Rhone

So many performers and recordings are credited with helping to introduce reggae music to the international mainstream that is often easy to forget the role played by one of the most pivotal movies of the 1970s. At a time when "popular" music and celluloid were still circling one another uneasily, with the importance of one always sublimated by the self-importance of the other (concert movies on the one hand, "let's put the show on here"–type teen flicks on the other), *The Harder They Come* bucked both trends by serving up a hard-hitting gangster film whose sparkling soundtrack was as integral to the plot as any other piece of action.

The handiwork of writer/director Perry Henzell, *The Harder They Come* was loosely based on the life and crimes of Ivanhoe "Rhygin" Martin, an outlaw in late-1940s Kingston whose escapades, and the legends that grew up around them, established him as a genuine folk hero among working-class Jamaicans. Anybody seeking a blueprint for the rude-boy lifestyle of the mid-1960s needed look no further than Martin, as Prince Buster proved when he scored a hit with the compulsive instrumental "Rhygin"—an unashamed tribute to the original rudie.

The story was updated, however; now Martin (Cliff) was an aspiring songwriter trying to make his way through the tangled undergrowth of the Kingston music scene, a world where a promise was no more reliable than the person who uttered it, nor a contract worth more than the man who signed it. A country boy, Martin is following his dreams, but reality is beyond his worst nightmares as he lurches from confidence trickster to gangster, and is left beaten, bloodied, and broke. When he falls in love, it's with a girl whose preacherman father cannot stand the sight of him.

It's a violent film, a depressing one in many ways, and it was a salutary one too, especially for any viewer who wanted to break into reggae music. It has also been described as positively the last image of Jamaica that the authorities would have wanted to see at a time when they were working hard to build up the country's tourism potential.

A decade had passed since James Bond's ***Dr. No*** had almost singlehandedly kicked off the newly independent island's vacation industry, with its sun, sea, sand, and glamour back-dropping Bond's stylish spy dramas. Now here was *The Harder They Come* painting the ghettos and slums as vividly as Bond portrayed the beaches, and even the scantily clad maidens whom the holiday brochures insisted were waiting to greet the lucky tourist were now revealed to be as sharklike as their ganja-smoking, gun-toting menfolk.

Happy holidays.

The movie is sensational, and the soundtrack is just as good. Overseen by producer Leslie Kong, his last major project before his tragically early death, it necessarily featured a lot of Jimmy Cliff—he and Kong had been working together long before Anglo-American fame grasped the singer. But the Melodians, the Maytals, Desmond Dekker, the Slickers, and the then-rising star of **DJ Scotty** were also involved, and the music they provided matches Cliff's almost blow for blow.

ROCKERS (1978)

Starring: ***Leroy "Horsemouth" Wallace,*** *Richard "Dirty Harry" Hall,* ***Jacob Miller****, Gregory Isaacs, Burning Spear,* ***Kiddus I****, Leroy Smart, Big Youth, Dillinger*

Directed and written by Theodorus Bafaloukos; produced by Patrick Hulsey

If any single movie can be said to not only encapsulate, but also epitomize, a moment in time in Jamaican culture, it is *Rockers*. In many ways, it follows *The Harder They Come* into the labyrinthine complexities of the local music industry; but it becomes very clear, very early on, that the fictions that gave the earlier movie its drive have been replaced here by realities—an impression that is heightened by the presence of so many contemporary musicians all but playing themselves.

Indeed, it comes as no surprise to learn that writer Bafaloukos originally intended *Rockers* to be a documentary, and it is the elements retained from that early scheme that lend so much dynamism to the finished fiction. Leroy Wallace's character even lives in Wallace's own home, with his own wife and children, while Inner Circle take a delightful potshot at their beginnings on the tourism circuit by appearing as the house band at an expensive hotel, and baffling the vacationers with an impassioned version of "Tenement Yard."

Wallace is the star of the movie, playing a drummer who earns a little extra cash by working as a bicycle messenger, delivering records from the studios to the stores. It should be an easy task but, of course, it soon turns out to be quite the opposite, as rival operators and avaricious outsiders step in to derail his journeys. Finally Wallace and his musician friends have had enough, and set about robbing the robbers who are choking their trade.

Deliberately and otherwise, *Rockers* is a lighthearted movie, the action rocking along in the arms of a positively delirious soundtrack. The cast gives an indication of what you can expect to hear as the movie goes along, and the soundtrack album that inevitably accompanied it stands as one of the best single-disc compilations of roots reggae on the market.

From the lightweight pop of Inner Circle to the instrumental virtuosity of the Rockers All Stars, the movie's themes are further mirrored by the use of Junior Murvin's "Police and Thieves," Jacob Miller's "Tenement Yard," and Gregory Isaacs's "Slave Master." Burning Spear, Kiddus I's "Graduation in Zion," and Third World's cover of "Satta Massagana" further the Rastafarian message, while Bunny Wailer's theme song and a well-placed flash of Peter Tosh's "Steppin' Razor" are highlights of their own.

COUNTRYMAN (1982)

Starring: Countryman, Hiram Keller, Carl Bradshaw, Basil Keane, Freshey Richardson
Directed by Dickie Jobson; executive produced by Stephane Sperry; produced by Chris Blackwell; art direction by Bernard Leonard; musical supervision by ***Wally Badarou***

If the heart of *The Harder They Come* and *Rockers* lay in the tortured corruption of the inner city, the soul of *Countryman* lay in the mystic purity of the interior, the mountains and hills that sit at the center of both Jamaica's most potent folklore and rich society's most enduring nightmare—that of the man from the hills, the untamed wild man unfettered by law or social mores, the primal energy that lurks in the darkness where civilization meets the wilderness.

In fact, **Countryman** was a Rastafarian philosopher, a friend of Bob Marley's and many other musicians too, and he had already been immortalized in one of Marley's most accomplished compositions, "Knotty Dread." But truth and mythology tend to blur in the mountains, and they blurred in music, too. The image of "Natty Dread" (as Island Records insisted the song be retitled) as a righteous assault on the evils of Babylon remained an act of psychic terrorism that was itself at the root of roots music.

In many ways, *Countryman*, the movie, is a confused little thing. The plot revolves, very basically, around an American woman whose small plane crashes in the mountains. She is rescued by Countryman and nursed back to health, while rival political groups back in the city try to distort the circumstances of the crash, to further their own ends in an upcoming election. A whole tissue of lies is constructed in order to help gain an advantage in the hustings—everything from arms and drug smuggling to the CIA. All of which impacts Countryman's own life, throwing him into intrigues that he might never have even dreamed of in the past.

It is a fairly standard political thriller laced with the age-old conflict between city life and country dweller, but shot with an unerring eye for Jamaica's natural scenic beauty, and then beautified even further by the soundtrack. Wally Badarou oversaw the movie's musical content, and his own pulsating themes are sensational, electrified *nyahbinghi* that is breathtakingly evocative. Into this mix is then dropped a healthy dose of Bob Marley and the Wailers, but a well-chosen one too: "Rastaman Chant," "Natural Mystic," and "Jah Lives" spearhead an admirably spiritual atmosphere, while contributions by Britain's **Steel Pulse** and Aswad, too, prove welcome.

DANCEHALL QUEEN (1997)

Starring: Audrey Reid, Paul Campbell, Carl Bradshaw, Beenie Man, Lady Saw, ***Anthony B, Chevelle Franklyn***
Directed by Don Letts and Rick Elgood; written by Suzanne Fenn, Ed Wallace, and Don Letts; executive produced by Chris Blackwell and Dan Geneti; produced by Carolyn Pfeiffer

Don Letts started his musical life as the disc jockey at London's Roxy club, the center of the city's punk-rock universe in 1977, spinning reggae between the punk bands while he waited for the first punk records to be released. He briefly managed the Slits, and joined Johnny Rotten and Richard Branson in Jamaica when Virgin's Frontline label was being schemed.

From there he moved to ex-Clash man Mick Jones's Big Audio Dynamite, a proto-hip-hop/rock concern that flickered briefly but brilliantly in the mid- and late 1980s. But he was also a dedicated documentary maker, shooting the seminal *Punk Rock Movie* in 1977, and also handling a stream of music videos through the 1980s and beyond. *Dancehall Queen* was his major directorial debut, however, and do *not* be put off by the DVD cover's insistence that it is "a modern-day Cinderella story." Because it is, but it is so much more than that.

Chevelle Franklyn's title theme, a glorious piece of electro dancehall that sticks to your ears like glue, draws you in straight away. And the story follows the song, as street-vendor Marcia (Audrey Reid) looks to the dancehall dance competitions as a way of perhaps pulling herself and her children out of poverty.

Of course it isn't that easy; between her boyfriend Larry and the thuggish Priest, she has a family background that could have hamstrung Nijinsky. But she is determined to fight, and to win, and there is a generation-capturing song selection to die for that pounds through every minute she spends on the dance floor: **Bounty Killer**, **Grace Jones**, **Chaka Demus and Pliers**, **Sugar Minott**, Beenie Man, Lady Saw, and Anthony B are all either seen or heard (or both) across an album that is as essential a primer for 1990s Jamaican music as any reggae-movie soundtrack.

THIRD WORLD COP (1999)

Starring: Paul Campbell, Mark Danvers, Carl Bradshaw, Audrey Reid
Directed by Chris Browne; written by Chris Browne, Chris Salewicz, and Suzanne Fenn; executive produced by Chris Blackwell

Audrey Reid returns from *Dancehall Queen*; Carl Bradshaw returns from almost every movie on this list; and Sly and Robbie lead a thunderous soundtrack to a movie that seems half concerned with again capturing the unique fission of the Kingston underworld, and half resigned to acknowledging that it could have been made in almost any city in the industrialized world. Such is the internationality of modern organized crime.

Certainly the story scarcely deviates from the time-honored fable of the good cop (Paul Campbell) discovering that his former best friend (Mark Danvers) is now a bad guy, a key figure in Carl Bradshaw's gunrunning operation. Friendship battles duty as gangsters battle cops, and there are some great shootout scenes pinned down by the music: Beenie Man, Wally Badarou, and sundry young Marleys are all heard. But that is all they are. Forget crime being a generic issue, crime movies are as well; and ultimately *Third World Cop* is best watched on a Saturday night when all you really want is some shoot-'em-up drama.

It's still a lot of fun, though; and watched back to back with *The Harder They Come*, it's astonishing how much Kingston has changed.

SHOTTAS (2002)

Starring: Ky-Mani Marley, ***Spragga Benz****, Louie Rankin,*
Wyclef Jean*, Paul Campbell, J. R. Silvera, Carlton Grant Jr.*
Directed and written by Cessa Silvera

Anybody who wonders why this list eschews the lamentable *Rude Boy*, starring Beenie Man and an aging Jimmy Cliff in a 2004 drug-running disaster, should leave the room now. There never was (and one doubts there ever will be) a sequel to *The Harder They Come* but, if there had to be, *Shottas* comes close.

Titled for the patois term for a gangster...literally, someone who calls the shots ... it is nominally the story of a teenage gang (led by Silvera and Grant) on the streets of late 1970s Kingston, shooting and looting their way out of poverty. Twenty years later, Silvera's character—now played by **Ky-Mani Marley**—is back on the streets, newly deported from the United States, and reuniting with his old mate Biggs (Spragga Benz) and a total psycho named Mad Max (Paul Campbell), and ... well, shooting and looting some more.

It's a tough action movie, well shot and extraordinarily dramatic when it needs to be—grainy black-and-white sequences strike you out of nowhere; slow-mo death scenes and jump-cut fights up the tempo even further; and the punchy soundtrack swings from **Damien Marley**'s "Welcome to Jamrock" to Bob Marley's "Three Little Birds" via contributions from Bounty Killer, Little John, Inner Circle, Pinchers, Junior Cat, and, of course, Marley and Benz. Again, it's hard not to think that much of this movie could have been shot anywhere, but Kingston lays down a suitably gritty backdrop to the best of the action, and that soundtrack is always going to keep things real.

Black Uhuru's storming *Sinsemilla* album. (Author's collection)

15

GUESS THEY'RE COMING TO DINNER: THE BEST OF BLACK UHURU

It is one of history's ironies that the bigger Bob Marley grew on an international scale, so did his Jamaican star fade, at least in terms of chart successes. Nobody denied his importance or his relevance. But the Wailers were spending much of their time away from the island, touring albums that seemed increasingly targeted toward the band's European, American, and Japanese following. New talents were thus constantly vying for their crown: Inner Circle, Third World, the Wailing Souls, and more.

There was competition, too, from within the Wailers' own family circle as Peter Tosh and Bunny Wailer both commenced their own solo careers, and the former at least grasped all the militant anger that had once been among the band's most potent calling cards and channeled it into his own music.

Black Uhuru would sweep them all to one side.

Certainly the band was a phenomenon. When they visited the U.K. in 1982, the opening act on the Rolling Stones' latest outing, they set the performance bar so high that everyone else really had to work hard to surpass them. The previous year had seen no fewer than three of the band's albums break into the U.K. chart; and two years later, their ***Anthem*** album became the first-ever victor in the Grammy Awards' newly instituted Best Reggae Album category.

And in between times, the so-called "classic" Black Uhuru lineup, led by vocalist Michael Rose and underpinned by the rhythm section of Sly and Robbie, could not put a foot wrong. But the breakup of that lineup, sparked at least in part by the musicians' frustration at not being able to make the final major breakthrough that their supporters deemed inevitable instead saw them slip back, and today we merely remember Black Uhuru. Had events transpired differently, we might have been worshipping them.

Black Uhuru started life as the vocal trio Uhuru (Swahili for "freedom") in the mid-1970s, debuting with a sweet cover of Curtis Mayfield's "Romancing to the Folk Song," but breaking up piecemeal when nothing really happened, leaving only vocalist **Duckie Simpson** to continue the vision. (Of his original bandmates, **Garth Dennis** joined the Wailing Souls, and Don Carlos went solo).

The errant pair were replaced by former **Jayes** frontman **Errol Nelson**, and Rose, a friend of drummer Sly Dunbar, with whom he had already recorded a version of what would become one of Black Uhuru's signature hits, "Guess Who's Coming to Dinner." For now, the new group realigned itself as Black Sounds Uhuru, and recorded the album ***Love Crisis*** with producer Prince Jammy in 1977 (a dub version, *Jammy's in Lion Dub Style*, later appeared), together with well-received covers of Bob Marley's "Natural Mystic" and "The Sun Is Shining." But it was another Rose composition, "I Love King Selassie," that proved the blueprint for the band's future; and with Nelson having been replaced by American born Sandra "Puma" Jones, the newly renamed Black Uhuru collaborated with Sly and Robbie's Taxi label and set about unleashing a succession of instant classics.

"General Penitentiary," "Guess Who's Coming to Dinner," "Plastic Smile," "Abortion," and "Shine Eye Gal" were machine-gunned into the market during 1978–1979 (Keith Richards dropped by to lace guest guitar across the last). A new album, aptly titled ***Showcase***, followed; and in 1980, Black Uhuru were the stars of the annual Reggae Sunsplash festival. Further singles "Wood for My Fire," "Rent Man," and "Observe Life" followed, and now Island Records swooped. Months later, the deathless ***Sinsemilla*** album formally introduced Black Uhuru to the international audiences whom they would court for the next five years.

SLY AND ROBBIE GO FREGGAE

Sly Dunbar and Robbie Shakespeare were largely still unknown outside of Jamaica when Island boss Chris Blackwell, who signed a distribution deal with their Taxi label in 1980, recruited them to lay down the backbeat behind funk singer Grace Jones, and in the process blueprint a large part of the early 1980s New York New Wave scene.

They followed this by pairing with English performer Ian Dury for his 1981 *Lord Upminster* album; and over the next few years Sly and Robbie were ubiquitous, recording with artists as far afield as Dylan, Barry Reynolds, Joe Cocker, Robert Palmer, Herbie Hancock (on his U.S. dance-chart smash "Rockit"), and Rolling Stone Mick Jagger.

Perhaps their most unexpected gig, however, came long before any of this, when they were recruited to cut an album, ***Aux Armes et Caetera***, with veteran French vocalist Serge Gainsbourg. The self-styled *enfant terrible* of French showbiz, Gainsbourg had cut a string of often-controversial records over the past twenty years, including such now-legendary assaults as "Lemon Incest," "Nazi Rock," and "Je T'Aime, Moi Non Plus," a sweet slice of orchestral melody with Gainsbourg and wife Jane Birkin moaning and groaning over the top. Now, however, he was planning his most audacious move yet, misappropriating the lyrics to the French national anthem and layering them over a reggae backdrop.

Gainsbourg had toyed with reggae in the past, with "Marilou Reggae" in 1976 (from the LP *L'Homme à Tête de Chou*). This time, however, he was no longer playing. Sending his artistic director Philippe Lerichomme out to buy a stack of recent reggae albums, Gainsbourg combed through them in search of the best musicians and best studio for his scheme. He settled, hardly surprisingly, on Dynamic Sounds Studios in Kingston, and Sly and Robbie.

The studio was booked for a week in September 1978, but it was an uneasy partnership to begin with. Gainsbourg had just celebrated his fiftieth birthday; and when the musicians gathered together by Sly and Robbie looked at the old man in the expensive suit, all wondered what on earth they had gotten themselves involved in.

Matters only worsened when Gainsbourg asked if they knew any French music. The whole room burst out laughing; but once the merriment had subsided, Dunbar acknowledged that they liked one song, an old instrumental with a woman groaning orgasmically over the string section. It was Gainsbourg's own "Je T'Aime, Moi Non Plus."

The sessions relaxed after that, all the more so once the band (which also included Bob Marley's wife Rita, and her vocal trio I-Threes) realized that Gainsbourg wanted the album to sound as authentically Jamaican as possible. There would be no overdubbing, no cleaning things up or smoothing them over. What the band played was what Gainsbourg sang over—rough, raw, and real. Which also summed up what he sang.

The assault on "La Marseillaise" was followed by "Relax Baby, Be Cool," a romantic come-on set against a race war in the American South. "Eau et Gaz à Tous les Étages" is the story of a man who takes out his penis and climbs the stairs of an apartment building, pissing and farting on every landing (the title translates as "Water and Gas on Every Floor"); and "Lola Rastaquouère" extolled the virtues, and the breasts, of an underage Rasta girl. Elsewhere, Gainsbourg revived one of his early 1960s numbers, "Javanaise," and revisited "Marilou Reggae." There was even a song about his recently deceased dog, Nana.

Beneath it all, Sly and Robbie percolated; above it all, the I-Threes chimed sweet harmonies, and *Aux Armes et Caetera* became Gainsbourg's biggest hit ever, going platinum in France and launching him into one of the biggest controversies of his career as the French Right Wing lined up against the mutilation of the anthem.

Newspaper headlines condemned him; and, when Gainsbourg toured France with Sly and Robbie again in attendance, bomb and death threats followed them everywhere. Indeed, the Strasbourg show was besieged by so many warnings that Gainsbourg gave the band the night off, and took the stage alone. There he performed "La Marseillaise" in its true form for an audience that seemed to be comprised wholly of militant right-wingers; then, as they stared in confusion, he offered them the rudest hand-and-arm gesture in the language, and left the stage.

But an exhilarating live album, ***Au Théâtre le Palace 1979***, caught the full band in full flight in Paris; and in 1981, the team reconvened at Compass Point in the Bahamas to record Gainsbourg's second reggae (or "freggae," as he insisted on calling it) album.

Mauvaises Nouvelles des Étoiles is a very different beast than its predecessor; Sly and Robbie had moved on in the world since their last encounter with Gainsbourg, accustoming themselves to better studios, better standards. No longer the raw power that had blasted behind Peter Tosh and, indeed, Gainsbourg in the past, they had tasted success with Black Uhuru and demand with Grace Jones *et al*. Gainsbourg is the unpolished diamond on this album, his disheveled cigarette-flavored vocal almost slumming it alongside the slick musicianship that accompanies him. The fart-heavy "Eugenie Sokolov" (titled for Gainsbourg's recently published novella) sounds especially at odds with everything else that is going on in the studio. It's still a great album; it's not just as great as *Aux Armes et Caetera*.

Both of Gainsbourg's freggae albums are essential, then, either in their original form, or spread across the double-disc deluxe editions that were released in France in 2003. These expanded collections serve up not only the albums, but also a disc apiece of often-radical dub versions cut in 2003, and a clutch of DJ versions too. Side by side, and spread across the four discs, freggae becomes as great a force to be reckoned with as Sly and Robbie themselves.

Red, home to the "Sponji Reggae" single, quickly followed; *Showcase* gained a much-welcomed international release, and with the Rolling Stones tour beckoning, ***Chill Out*** topped off this period with Black Uhuru's fourth drop-dead classic album. Touring with Sly and Robbie, guitarists Darryl Thompson and Mikey Chung, keyboard player Keith Sterling, and percussionist Sly Juice, Black Uhuru were at their peak, a point proven by the live ***Tear It Up*** album, a disc that still stands alongside the Wailers' and the Maytals' *Live* sets as essential mementos of roots at its in-concert finest.

Hindsight says the group should have continued hitting hard. Instead, a year would pass before Black Uhuru resurfaced, the hiatus interrupted only by the oddly unsatisfying *Dub Factor* collection and a fast-escalating chain of outside engagements for Sly and Robbie. The self-styled Riddim Twins were probably the most in-demand session team of the decade, and Black Uhuru suffered in their absence.

The latest seismic shifts on the home front, too, affected the band. Elsewhere around the world, the most popular reggae artists were measured by their LPs. In Jamaica, however, the single continued to rule supreme. One song, three minutes, 45 rpm, and it really didn't matter who the performer was, so long as the record got everybody dancing.

The increasing introspection of roots reggae, even when pounded out as joyously as the best of Black Uhuru, rarely hit that button; and a new wave of performers for whom the dance was again the defining goal began arising. **Barrington Levy**, **Johnny Osbourne**, Sugar Minott, and Frankie Paul emerged as defining vocal stylists; **Yellowman**, Eek-A-Mouse, and **Toyan** headed up a new wave of DJs. The cultural themes of old were thrown aside; the dancehalls returned to their old predilection for coarse sexuality and brute humor. The slacker generation was here, and as computer technology weighed in too, the sounds of Black Uhuru suddenly seemed old-fashioned.

Ragga erupted, pioneered by Sly and Robbie's own relentless ambition and curiosity, and led by Bounty Killer, **Shaggy**, Chaka Demus and Pliers, and Shabba Ranks. Beenie Man, **Buju Banton**, Sizzla, and **Elephant Man** emerged to take the world by storm. And they did so with a musical ruthlessness that no Jamaican export had ever before displayed. Merging with other, international, musical fields—predominantly hip-hop in the U.S.—the early 1990s saw the music finally complete the hybrid that the earliest Jamaican musicians, as they married their mento to imported R&B, had been dreaming of. And the past was left far behind.

Black Uhuru's *Anthem*, in 1984, was one of the first major releases to illustrate the gulf that was suddenly forming between the demands of the Jamaican market and those of a more international audience. A little over a decade before, Chris Blackwell had completely remixed and overdubbed the Wailers' first Island Records album in hopes of luring in rock audiences through the back door. All these years later, and the same games were still being played, a point proven by the album's inclusion of a so-faithful version of Sly Stone's "Somebody's Watching You."

The album itself was remixed and re-sequenced for European and U.S. release. And while the short-term advantages included that Grammy triumph, it was a pyrrhic victory. Michael Rose left the band (he was replaced by **Junior Reid**); the group departed Island Records; and all the momentum of the past half a decade was lost. When the Black Uhuru story was anthologized on the two-CD *Liberation* compilation, *Anthem* was represented only by the original Jamaican mixes. The westernized takes were expunged from history.

The group would continue, and a Black Uhuru still exists, led as ever by Duckie Simpson. But little of their post-Rose output, a catalogue that now embraces two decades of music, can touch the heights that the band once danced upon; and the passing of time has not been kind to it, either. Return, however, to that sequence of albums that chased them from *Showcase* to *Chill Out*, and was topped off by that so-seismic live album, and Black Uhuru again have no peers.

Roddy Radiation's Skabilly Rebels—as special as the Specials! (Author's collection)

16

SOME SPECIAL MADNESS: THE WORLD TURNS 2-TONE

Home and abroad, the late 1970s were a blazing ferment of idealism and danceability, the twin energies of punk and reggae clashing with such resonance that it was inevitable that the ensuing hybrid would shatter skulls. An inevitability that was seized upon by the Specials.

Starting life as the Automatics, the band was formed in Coventry, in the English midlands, in 1978; in spring 1979, the Specials scored a monster hit with their very first record, "Gangsters." It was a self-released mash of frenetic rhythms and screeching brakes, Prince Buster intonations, and compulsive dance. By the time the original group broke up in late 1981, the Specials hadn't simply established themselves among the U.K.'s most successful bands, they had also ignited an entire new musical hybrid, the sound of 2-Tone.

The Specials' modus operandi, and that of the bands that were to follow them, was simple: a vibrant reinvention tying old-time ska rhythms to punk attack, taking messages that made sense in the 1960s and allowing them to live again in the early 1980s. Nor, although the era of true 2-Tone mania seemed to elapse in a matter of months, was it a passing phase.

Madness, the English Beat, Bad Manners, and the Selecter all grew from the soil that the Specials so exuberantly tilled, while an entire forest of new acts emerged from the Specials' own family tree—Terry Hall's Fun Boy Three and Colourfield; Jerry Dammers's the Special AKA; Special Beat; and so many more. Today, the Specials' own members are granted the same venerable-veteran status as any of the Jamaican stars they listened to in childhood. Yet they are also responsible for some of the most fascinating artistic hybrids that the original music has ever yielded.

Terry Hall's 2003 partnership with Fun-Da-Mental's Mushtaq, for example, unleashed *The Hour of Blue Light*, an album of world-music stylings and rhythms that is as fascinating in its surprises as his union with **Dub Pistols**; Hall and the Pistols enjoyed a musical homecoming across their *Speakers and Tweeters* CD. Likewise his bandmates, as their own careers have taken them through their own tales of the musically unexpected.

Few, however, strayed so far from the path, while at the same time as remaining faithfully true to it, as **Roddy Radiation**, the Specials' guitar player. Leaf through any rock-history book, after all, and chances are Radiation is best remembered for his career with that band alone—whether the first time around or via the reunions of the 1990s and beyond. The soul of his career, however, were the years that were bookended by those skanking glories, building around a unique and ferociously reinterpreted brand of rockabilly—much of which was highlighted on the ***Skabilly Rebel: The Roddy Radiation Anthology*** CD.

Comprising twenty tracks drawn from almost as many years' worth of unreleased demos, outtakes, and sessions, *Skabilly Rebel* serves up bone-shaking highlights of each of the bands that Radiation had led since the 1981 demise of the Specials: the Tearjerkers, the Bonediggers, and the Raiders. In addition, a clutch of demos recorded both solo and in cahoots with his brother Mark Byers, plus a solitary outtake from the Specials' 1996 reincarnation, completed a portrait that adds up to one of the most singularly satisfying albums yet released under the fast-devaluing banner of "anthology."

The fact that it accomplishes all this without resorting to any of Radiation's own so-called "greatest hits" only amplifies said achievement. This is the man who wrote "Rat Race," "Holiday Fortnight," and "Hey Little Rich Girl." In ska-land, he's a legend. But *Skabilly Rebel* is a new world of its own, and it might even be more fun.

The son of a soul-band trumpeter, Roddy "Radiation" Byers's first instrument was trombone before he switched to guitar at thirteen and began the traditional apprenticeship through the local youth-club circuit. By 1977, Radiation was a member of the regional punk group the Wild Boys, then joined another outfit, the Automatics, after an evening out with that band's founder, Jerry Dammers. "He said that they were going to London the next day to record some demos; and did I want to play guitar at the session? I said, 'Yes,' got drunk, went home, and forgot all about it—until they turned up at my house the next morning, banging on the front door while I was still in bed. 'Fuck me! They meant it!'"

The Automatics became the Specials in early 1978; a year later, completely redesigned around a sharp-suited, tightly coiled ska-punk hybrid, the band scored its first hit with "Gangsters," sending half the Western world 2-Tone crazy.

"I really enjoyed their energy," Joe Strummer mused later. "A lot of bands were doing the punk-reggae thing at that time, us included, but they were taking it all very seriously, very rootsy. The [Specials], though, had a really different approach, which was down to a lot of things, but mainly, I think, Terry's voice. He didn't have a reggae voice, and he didn't even try. He sounded so English, and that was the difference."

From the outset, however, the band members' own musical tastes were at odds with the Specials' best-known specialties; Dammers was the ska fan, his bandmates' interests ranged far wider, and touring the U.S. in early 1980 gave Radiation the opportunity to stretch his musical wings—stylistically if not yet musically. He recalls, "[Jerry Dammers] said I came back looking like Marlon Brando circa *The Wild One*. I'd suddenly discovered that I could get all the gear I ever wanted in American thrift shops—leathers, cowboy shirts, hats, and motorbike boots, Marlon Brando, James Dean. I also started getting into rockabilly in a big way. I'd always liked the music, but now it became my religion. The music being played on the tour bus would usually be heavy reggae or jazz, which after several weeks would fail to excite me. So I started putting my own records on."

By the end of 1980, the Specials were over. Although the group would theoretically survive into the following summer, and score a forever-memorable U.K. #1 with their final single, "Ghost Town," they were united "in name only," as Radiation puts it. Bandmates Terry Hall, **Lynval Golding**, and **Neville Staples** were already scheming their own group, the Fun Boy Three; in early 1981, Radiation followed suit and formed the Tearjerkers.

FIFTY SKA AND 2-TONE CLASSICS (AND ONE EP), 1979–1981

"A Message to You, Rudy"—The Specials

"Apache"—**The Ska-Dows**

"Babylon's Burning"—The Ruts

"Baggy Trousers"—Madness

"Big Fat Man"—Laurel Aitken

"Can Can"—Bad Manners

"Do Nothing"—The Specials

"Doors of Your Heart"—The Beat

"Drowning"—The Beat

"Easy Life"—**The Bodysnatchers**

"Elvis Should Play Ska"—Graduate

"Embarrassment"—Madness

"Gangsters"—The Specials

"Ghost Town"—The Specials

"Hands Off She's Mine"—The Beat

"I Like Bluebeat"—**Cairo**

"Jah War"—The Ruts

"Let's Do Rocksteady"—The Bodysnatchers

"Lip Up Fatty"—Bad Manners

"Lorraine"—Bad Manners

"Lovers Rock"—Judge Dread

"Missing Words"—The Selecter

"My Girl"—Madness

"Ne Ne Na Na Na Na Nu Nu"—Bad Manners

"On My Radio"—The Selecter
"One Step Beyond"—Madness
"Phoenix City"—**Rockers Express**
"Please Play My Record"—**Arthur Kay's Originals**
"The Prince"—Madness
"Rat Race"—The Specials
"Rude Boys Are Back in Town"—**Boff**
"Rudi Got Married"—Laurel Aitken
"Rudi the Red Nose Reindeer"—**The Gangsters**
"Saturday Night Beneath the Plastic Palm Trees"—**Leyton Buzzards**
"Sea Cruise"—Rico
"The Selecter"—The Selecter
"Ska Trekkin'"—**The Tigers**
"Ska Wars"—Arthur Kay's Originals
"Ska'd for Life"—**Akrylykz**
"South Coast Rumble"—**The South Coast Ska Stars**
The Special AKA Live! EP—The Specials
"Special Brew"—Bad Manners
"Stand Down Margaret"—The Beat
"Staring at the Rude Boys"—The Ruts
"Stereotypes (Part One)"—The Specials
"Tears of a Clown"—The Beat
"Telstar"—The Ska-Dows
"Three Minute Hero"—The Selecter
"Time Is Tight"—**The Ska City Rockers**
"Too Much Pressure"—The Selecter
"Too Nice to Talk To"—The Beat

The Tearjerkers (no relation to the similarly named Irish band who gigged around the U.K. a year or two before) delved deep into the soul of Radiation's beloved rockabilly, dramatically melding it with the Specials' own ska beat in a fusion that was promptly labelled "skabilly," of course. Radiation told *The Face* magazine, "Black and white players borrow ideas from each other, and the hybrid[ized] ideas are the key to musical progression. So I mixed my two favorite styles, and hey, presto!"

Indeed, the Specials' Radiation-powered forays in that direction notwithstanding, rockabilly and ska might well have been the only two major musical genres that had *not* been intermixed in recent years, and that despite the combination not only making musical sense, but being historically logical as well. Trace back to the earliest days of ska in Jamaica, and American rockabilly records were one of the primal reference points for many of the new style's pioneers.

Reinventing that fission in 1981, at a time when the now-rampant rockabilly stylings of the Stray Cats and the fast-emerging Polecats were pushing what looked like another full-scale revival into the chart, only the Tearjerkers' distinctly part-time nature seemed set to prevent them from following the leaders to instant glory. That, however, did not overly concern Radiation. For him, it was enough, simply, that the band existed.

"I needed an outlet for my many new songs, and enjoyed being my own boss in my own band," Radiation recalls. Many of these songs appeared for the first time on *Skabilly Rebel*; although the Tearjerkers remained a major live draw around the U.K. for much of the next five years, the group released no more than one single, when "Desire" appeared on the Chiswick label during 1982. (Interestingly, Radiation originally offered the record to the Specials' own 2-Tone label. He remembers: "I asked Jerry at a party about releasing it, and he head-butted a wall.")

Despite their vinyl silence, the Tearjerkers made some memorable live appearances. They supported Elvis Costello at the Southend Pavilion, and tore up the London Venue when they opened there for Dave Edmunds. They scoured the U.K. alongside punk heroes Stiff Little Fingers, and were a highlight of the now-legendary The Good the Bad and the Ugly tour in 1982 alongside the Bureau and the Modettes. ("I don't remember which order that was in," Radiation laughs.) The Tearjerkers were also regulars at Rock Against Racism benefit shows, "and usually anything for a good cause. I always found it hard saying no. The list goes on and on . . . I remember we did a really good BBC Radio *In Concert* with Wilko Johnson . . ."

Not until 1987 did this hardworking group finally run its course, after which Radiation tried working solo for a couple of years. By 1990, however, he was looking to return to the band format once again, and formed the Bonediggers. Again, however, the live circuit alone sustained them; and, by 1994, having already slimmed down into the three-piece Raiders, the end was nigh.

The Raiders broke up, but Radiation continues: "Shortly after the band split, I was asked to back Desmond Dekker with some of the Specials—Horace Panter, Lynval Golding, and Neville Staples, plus 'H' from the Selecter on drums. It turned out to be fun; and when Lynval approached me to play a tour of Japan as the Specials Mark One, singing lead vocals, I agreed. At the time, no one considered it a long-term project, but following Japan, we were offered some festivals in Europe; the USA started beckoning, and suddenly it was all starting again."

Over the next four years, the renewed Specials toured constantly, and recorded a couple of albums—the all-covers ***Today's Specials***, and the originals-heavy ***Guilty Until Proven Innocent***. Radiation reflects fondly upon that latter release, at least: "Some of the new tunes on there were as good, if not better, than the Specials Mark One. But the press backlash, and the fact that the old stuff was still available—and five dollars or more cheaper—meant it never received a proper listening."

No matter. The band had utterly transformed itself from riotous nostalgia to cutting-edge efficiency. When they played WBCN's Christmas Rave in 1997, the *Boston Globe* gushed, "The new material was consistent with their skanking gems from the late '70s." And Horace Panter acknowledged all that had conspired to make the reunion as successful as the first time around when he said, "Bands like **No Doubt**, **Goldfinger**, and the Toasters have made it known to us that they were inspired by our music, and we appreciate the fact that they acknowledge us. The ska scene has always been sort of grassroots. It was always about integrity. Bands support each other . . . that's what 2-Tone is all about."

Sadly, the new group was not built to last. "Thousands of new Specials fans proved the band still meant something," says Radiation. "Unfortunately, even though we were all older, it seemed we were no wiser. Differences in direction and the usual petty squabbles split the band."

Radiation, however, had already seen the end coming during 1997. Even before the Specials broke up, he was pushing a new band into action, **the Skabilly Rebels**, and designing a new image that, in its own way, was as potent as the 2-Tone stylings that had attended his earlier group.

"I was thinking of logos for the new band, and I spotted some kids in the audience [at a Specials concert in the U.S.] wearing Skatalites T-shirts with the Jamaican flag as a logo. I noticed the crossbar design was similar to the old Confederate rebel flag; and, in a moment of madness, I thought: *If I combine the two designs, it would be a combination of ska-reggae and rock 'n' roll*—which, in Britain, is represented by the stars and bars. I asked my black friends if this would be a problem—they said, 'No, but the KKK might not dig it!' Which suits me fine."

Trojan Records—a trademark of quality. (Author's collection)

17

HAPPY TOGETHER: ROCKING STEADY WITH FLO & EDDIE

A pair of bored Los Angeles children's-television writers whose musical career had seen them provide backing vocals for Frank Zappa, Marc Bolan, and Alice Cooper probably isn't the first place one would look for an unknown reggae classic. America was scarcely fertile ground for reggae music even after Bob Marley's breakthrough, with the general public more likely to associate the music with the English Beat than Lee Perry—and the likes of the Specials and Madness (chartbusters almost everywhere else on the planet) still confined to a tiny box marked "cult."

So no. Move along. There is nothing to see or listen to here.

Or is there? Those two television writers. What if they had also one been the quintessential sound of the American sixties, the voices that powered the Turtles to stardom, at precisely the same time as Jamaica's rocksteady movement was likewise built upon the passion of vocal harmony? And what if they had also spent enough time in Europe to have thoroughly assimilated the reggae sounds that regularly infiltrated the British chart?

And what if…

"When you had a slow day writing stupid scripts for elephants to sing, then 'you could roll a big one, mon' and kick back and listen to the I-Threes, Peter Tosh; or listen to Gregory Isaacs; or listen to Dennis Brown; or listen to Augustus Pablo, any of the people that were coming into our realm then."

THE ULTIMATE INTERACTIVE GUIDE TO MARIJUANA

You probably don't even have a computer capable of running the game any longer. But if you cast your mind back to the early days of computer games, you might also be able to absorb yourself in what was, for a few months in 1999, the ultimate in digital play.

The basic premise of *The Ultimate Interactive Guide to Marijuana* was simple. *This* was your brain. *This* was your brain on drugs. And *this* was your brain as it came to grips with a CD-ROM that was truly the most fun you could have without inhaling, and probably even more than that.

The game itself was simplicity: staking out a five-room hippie pad, picking up sundry drug paraphernalia (rolling papers, ashtrays ...), and earning enough hash-brownie points to enter the chill-out room. In between times, a ripping electro-dub soundtrack kept you buzzing, skittering insects (roaches—get it?) kept you hopping, and every so often you'd click on a wotsit that fed your head with useful information. Such as comparative sentences for marijuana possession around the world and the relative potency of popular plants; there was even a high-tech version of the kids' game *Operation*, documenting the health risks and benefits of smoking reefer.

Articles from the dope-fiend bible *High Times*, how to (or not) tips and comments, suggestions for things you could do with hemp that don't involve getting high (it makes great paper, clothes, and rope), and some truly fabulous graphics and art confirmed *The Ultimate Interactive Guide to Marijuana* as one of the most entertaining ROMs of its era. Today, well, the graphics look primitive, the action is slow, and it all feels rather clunky and dull. But roll another big one, mon, and it catapults you to places you might never want to leave.

Howard Kaylan and Mark Volman, AKA **Flo & Eddie**, AKA the Phlorescent Leech & Eddie, already had a proud heritage. The Turtles' "Happy Together" and "Elenore" surely rank among the greatest pop records ever made, while their work as session men for, indeed, Zappa, Bolan, Alice, and many more had established their vocals among the most instantly recognizable of the 1970s.

But they were always looking for new thrills; and when news of the 2-Tone movement made its way across the Atlantic, the two self-confessed Anglophiles were instantly intrigued. Kaylan explains, "We were hearing what we were being told was a huge movement over there. The reggae movement. So not knowing what the hell was truly going on, we started out with the Bob Marley records and we went through all of them. For two guys who'd had maybe three-and-a-half pounds of weed with them at any given time in the office, this was something we were destined to listen to."

Their tastes swiftly developed. "We were listening to people who were fringe even if you knew Jamaican music. I mean, if you didn't know specifically who the people were in the Syndicate of Sound, we didn't want you in the office. You weren't enough of a reggae aficionado for us. So we started listening to all of it, and we knew it backward and forward, and finally we came across this guy by the name of Warren Smith who owned a label called Epiphany and he was producing Jamaican records for Soul Syndicate and for other Jamaican artists and their backup bands. And he said, 'You know, you guys are very happy together, you should go in there with your voices, you'd make the ultimate reggae album.' We said, 'Yeah, that would be great, but who's going to pay for it?' He said, 'I will.'"

Smith was true to his word, and then some. Within weeks of the meeting, Flo & Eddie had new identities, Prince Flo and Jah Edward I, and were ensconced in a Kingston hotel room, thrashing out a list of the songs they wanted to cover on their album. "A lot of which," Kaylan continues, "would be eliminated when we met up with Errol Brown, who would become our coproducer on the project. He came up with many more interesting songs, and also introduced us to a term we really didn't know, which was *rocksteady*.

"The entire term had been foreign to us; we didn't know what a rocksteady song meant, and that it referred to a particular type of love ballad. But it was a ballad that suited us, particularly my vocal stylings."

Brown immediately took the project in hand. The nephew of legendary producer Duke Reid, Brown was then involved in sorting through his kinsman's archives for remixes and reissues.

With his ear already attuned to the job, he singled out a wealth of veteran Jamaican gems that he thought the duo might turn to their advantage: undisputed classics such as the Melodians' "Swing and Dine," Ken Boothe's "Moving Away," Delroy Wilson's "Dancing Mood," the Heptones' "Party Time," the **Gaylads**' "Rock With Me Baby," **Delano Stewart**'s "Sitting in the Park," and Stranger and Gladdy's "Just Like a River."

The Prince and Jah Edward in turn volunteered just two songs from their original list: a reggaefied version of "Happy Together," and "Prisoner of Love," a 1940s-era Perry Como hit written by one of Volman's distant cousins, Leo Robin. "He'd written all sorts of great songs, 'Thanks for the Memories,' 'Love in Bloom'... everybody's theme song was written by that guy way back in the '30s or '40s, or whenever that was. 'Prisoner of Love' was a very schmaltzy tune; but worked up [in] reggae fashion, it was beautiful."

It was also a tune that Kaylan's parents considered "their song" and that he laughingly acknowledges that they had "spooned and crooned to while they were courting. To see the expressions on their faces when they heard our version of it was worth the price of admission. The last thing from me they had heard in earnest, I believe, was [Zappa's] 'Billy the Mountain,' and they weren't too thrilled. They weren't Zappa's fans; it was just sort of, 'My poor boy, my poor boy. What's happened to you?'"

The sessions proceeded absolutely painlessly, a happenstance that surprised the album's makers as much as anybody. Brown had assembled an amazing band for them to work with, top-line musicians like drummer Carlton "Santa" Davis; former Wailers bassist Aston "Family Man" Barrett; guitarist Earl "Chinna" Smith; keyboard player Augustus Pablo; and percussionist Uziah "Sticky" Thompson.

"So we were really excited about that. But we got there and discovered they had just had a real shitty experience, those very same players in that another white musician [a very famous one, we waspishly muse] had come to Jamaica to do some recording, had used all of the very same musicians, and had left the island without paying them. Perfect, right? We said, we want to come down and make a reggae album at your studio—they were like, 'Okay, great, another chance to get ripped off.'

"But instead, we came down there, the first thing we did was to ask where are these guys getting their weed, and they all pointed to this little hut at the back of Bob Marley's property that was Juicy's Hut. Juicy was a Rasta who lived on the property who made smoothies for everybody and who also did a bit of dealing, but only if you were staying or working at the studio. So we'd hit Juicy's hut up every day and buy everything he had, and lay it out on the console in the studio and say, 'Whoever wants it, there it is,' all day long, all night long. As long as you're recording, you're smoking.

"So word got out pretty quick, and people that weren't even supposed to be playing on the record showed up to play."

The raw recordings were astonishing, exceeding even the musicians' expectations. Kaylan admits, "I really expected the project to go south at some point, and turn into some sort of pop record, but we were able to keep it pure."

Even when the Kingston sessions ended, the team remained together. "We flew Errol and the other engineer people from Jamaica to Malibu, to California, with us, and we finished the vocals and we did the mixing there. And we kept it as true as we could to their style of mixing and to the genre, so we wouldn't be adding anything. Even the horn players that we brought in to record those parts were damned authentic, because they are equally high. I think.

"But they also understood the flavor of the project, and being true to it; and believe it or not, of all the things that I've recorded, ***Rock Steady with Flo & Eddie*** is still among my favorite projects. Certainly among my favorite Flo & Eddie projects. It is still so pure, and the sound is so sparse and satisfying to me, and since I like the sound of my own voice, evidently, to an inordinate degree, I really like that album."

He laughs. "For purists looking to find that rocksteady genre of recording, they would not suspect, perhaps from looking at the cover, that this is going to be a decent reggae record. But, in fact, it is."

From tiny skacore acorns, massive superstars did grow. (Author's collection)

18

THE HEAVY, HEAVY BOSSTONE SOUND: SKA IN AMERICA

Britain fell hard for 2-Tone, and the rest of the world was not slow to follow. And whereas British fancies soon toppled by the wayside, elsewhere the music proved to be fit for the long, long haul.

America's **the Untouchables**, **the Mighty Mighty Bosstones**, **the Toasters**, and No Doubt all formed during the early to mid-1980s to pursue their own love of the Specials' musical hybrid, and all did so with such success that, by the early 1990s, the entire U.S.A., it seemed, was skanking to a similar rhythm—a musical movement that was all the more glorious because absolutely nobody had expected it. You opened the music magazines of the day and it was all grunge, industrial, and Oasis-shaped Britpop. But then you went out to a club and it was wall-to-wall ska. And, for two or three glorious years, that's how it stayed.

America's ska movement, like its U.K. forebear, was birthed by punk but fermented by experience. Talking in the mid-1990s, at the peak of his band's success, Dicky Barrett of Boston's Mighty Mighty Bosstones explained, "I started my punk-rock life at eleven. I was the kid hiding in the clubs and getting thrown out. I was drunk a good portion of the time."

Music was crucial. Barrett continues, "I understood the Jam, I understood Madness, I loved the Ruts, I understood Sham 69 ... the first time I saw Johnny Rotten, he looked like an alien to my dad, but he looked really cool to me.

"If Bad Manners were coming to town, that was a month right there, planning what we were going to do, how's the day going to be planned. 'Okay, we'll meet the night before, we'll talk about it, play the records. What songs are they going to do?' And that's definitely something we've taken with us. We go to a city, we're here to entertain you, you've spent such and such an amount of money and we respect that and we want to give you something back."

YOUR MANNERS ARE DISGUSTING

Even under his real name of Doug Trendle, Buster Bloodvessel was always the world's most unlikely pop star. But Bad Manners were tailored for nothing less. Riotous, raucous, and remarkable even after you stopped pinching yourself in the hope you'd wake up, the nine-man, one-noise Manners came crashing out of the British ska scene at exactly the same time as Madness and the Specials, with the self-same agenda, and the same sense of style.

And all similarities ended right there.

Madness were the nutty boys; Bad Manners were totally insane. When they settled down and simply played, they created the smoothest ska sounds around, defiantly authentic, desperately beautiful. But settling down is what you do when you're old and gray with children and a mortgage, and who wants to spend an evening with their parents? Bad Manners kicked ass like teenagers kick cans—because they are there, because it is fun, and because they can. Lunatic solos were played strictly for laughs, and Buster himself—a man mountain in braces with rude, crude cropped hair and a lascivious paunch that wobbled when he skanked—was the chortling cheerleader who held the riot together.

Right from the start, and the opening chorus of their very first single, Bad Manners carved out their own corner. While other bands fell over each other to sign to the flagship 2-Tone label, Bad Manners struck out for the comparatively unfashionable Magnet. While other bands donned porkpie hats and sharp suits, Bad Manners wore T-shirts and turned-up jeans. And while other groups turned to the Jamaican greats for their earliest singles, Bad Manners turned to the nursery and emerged with the utterly irresistible "Ne Ne Na Na Na Na Nu Nu."

They followed it up with "Lip Up Fatty"; and by the time "Special Brew" gave them the biggest ska hit of 1981 (bar the Specials), Bad Manners were confirmed as the crown clown princes of monster ska lunacy. Even within the horn-blaring confines of the ska explosion, Bad Manners' first album, ***Ska'n'B***, hit with all the finesse of a fart in a funeral home. And though the mourners looked shocked, they couldn't help but laugh.

Through daring ska remakes of whatever song came to mind, Bad Manners went from "Monster Mash" to "The Magnificent Seven" with barely a pause for breath. Then just when you thought things could never get sillier, they dredged up "Scruffy Was a Huffy Chuffy Tug Boat" and lowered the common denominator even further. Again, it was total madness, but Madness were never this delightfully daft; and when detractors described them as a bunch of loonee tunes, Bad Manners snagged the insult for their second album title.

Crisscrossing the Atlantic for American tours that were, if anything, even wilder than their European jaunts, Bad Manners swiftly established themselves as the premier attraction on the local ska circuit. Their relationship with their American fans was based on precisely the same basic pretexts as that underpinning their rapport with their British followers: the group's manic exuberance, their devotion to the music, and an endless appetite for enduringly bad taste.

The difference was that as the 1980s pressed on, and the original 2-Tone scene began to break up, Bad Manners were one of the few old-school British ska bands who never even thought about changing. They knew, as their audience knew, that ska was more than a music, it was a total way of life; and they lived it to the limit.

There was method to their mayhem, too. If nobody took the band seriously, they would never have to, either. Other groups grew old and sensible, replacing childish lunacy with studied adult calmness. Bad Manners swore they'd never grow up, and the hit singles kept on coming. "Lorraine," "Just a Feeling," "Walking in the Sunshine," and best of all—the daftest of all—a traumatic ton-up smash 'n' grab through the confines of the "Can Can."

Nothing, not even a relatively faithful, joyously infectious rendition of the old Millie Small standard "My Boy Lollipop" (retitled, naturally, "My Girl Lollipop"), could ever top the "Can Can," and Bad Manners never even tried. A massed audience sing-along where the only words are "la la la," Bad Manners had gone all the way. And when the hits dried up in 1983, Buster & co. carried on regardless, and carried their audience with them.

In 1989, a full decade after the group first formed, they released ***Return of the Ugly***, one of the greatest ska albums ever recorded, and one of the most audacious. Laurel Aitken rubs shoulders with the theme from *Bonanza*; and the title track says more for Bad Manners than anyone else ever has.

The first band Barrett ever met up close and personal was Madness. "They played *Saturday Night Live*, and me and my friend Patrick got on a bus late at night, got into NYC early in the morning, had to stand in line all day for tickets, drank in an Irish pub somewhere really close to the NBC Studios, and ended up hanging out with guys who became members of the Toasters, and Django, who was in the **Stubborn All-Stars**. And after the show, we hung around outside waiting for Madness. And they spotted us, took us in their limo, let us hang out with them. Suggs was introducing me as his American cousin. If I hadn't been in the Bosstones afterward, it would have been the biggest musical thrill of my life."

But he *was* in the Bosstones and, throughout the 1990s, that band led a flying phalanx of ska-intoxicated punks whose output, across so many albums, remains as prodigious as any of the ska booms that preceded it.

The catalyst for all that was to come were the Toasters, a New York–based band whose birth was roughly contemporary with the death of the Specials in 1981, and whose original name more or less sums up mainstream American attitudes toward reggae. In the wide world outside of the ska clubs, reggae meant just one thing: Bob Marley. So frontman Bucket and his friends called themselves **Not Bob Marley** and allowed people to draw their own conclusions.

Not Bob Marley became the Toasters two years and one single later, recording what became their debut ***Recriminations*** EP with producer Joe Jackson, the New Wave wonder of recent renown. No label in America would touch it, however, so the band took another leaf out of the old Specials' manual, and formed their own. Moon Ska would go on to become *the* guiding light of American ska, responsible for releasing music by nigh on every significant band in the land—and beyond.

The label's earliest releases were understandably tentative, concentrating on singles and compilations highlighting the handful of other bands who shared the Toasters' ska fixation. The first, ***New York Beat***, naturally concentrated on their immediate locale. But as word of the band and the label spread, so other talents started to make themselves known. Beginning in Boston, where **Bim Skala Bim** had been around almost as long as the Toasters and were already riding a stunning self-titled debut album recorded with producer Jimmy Miller—best known for his late-1960s/early-1970s stint with the Rolling Stones.

More reggae-inflected than its ska-dancing brethren, *Bim Skala Bim* remains a phenomenal album, one of the finest American releases of the 1980s whatever the genre; but it was not to be alone for long. The Toasters' ***Thrill Me Up*** shares its manic delight in the music, a Mach Three demolition derby that dares even the most sedentary listener not to get up and dance. The fact that both bands were still at the starting gate in terms of what they would go on to achieve only amplifies these accomplishments.

The Bosstones, **the Cheapskates**, **Gangster Fun**, and more all followed; by the time Moon Ska unveiled the *Mashin' Up the Nation* compilation, they were sadly turning bands away—but keeping their contact info on hand. By the end of the 1980s, Moon Ska had not only outlived the 2-Tone label that inspired it, it had a potential roster of artists as large as any established major concern. And as the following decade approached *its* conclusion, ska, in all its possible permutations, was big news.

The Toasters scored their biggest hit yet with ***Don't Let the Bastards Grind You Down***, an LP that shifted from rootsy ska to classic '60s songs (a cover of the Spencer Davis Group classic "Gimme Some Lovin'") into jazz, funk, and swing. Moon Ska remained the titular figurehead of the entire musical movement, doing so despite the first major labels making their own moves into the scene (the Bosstones went to Mercury, **Less Than Jake** to Capitol, and **Save Ferris** to Epic). When ska erupted on the big screen, it was thanks to Moon Ska coordinating the soundtrack to the independent-movie sleeper *Bang*.

Elsewhere ...

Goldfinger seemed as ubiquitous as the British secret agent who once tried to rub out their namesake.

Reel Big Fish were real big.

The Hippos were being courted by every major in town, and selling up a storm with their ***Forget the World*** CD, while Stiff Dog labelmates **the Adjustments** were moving down to L.A. at the same time as they were moving up to the next level with the release of their brilliant (and brilliantly titled) ***Everybody Must Get Cloned*** debut album.

And hanging over them all, a California band called No Doubt.

It was, inevitably, Moon Ska that launched No Doubt onto the national stage. Although the band had been around the California ska scene since the early 1980s, it was the dawn of the next decade before they were highlighted on a wider level with the release of Moon Ska's 1992 ***California Ska-Quake*** compilation.

Four years earlier, the same label released ***Skaface***, a set inspired by the sheer weight of local scenes that the Toasters discovered when they visited California during their *Skaboom!* tour. It remains a dynamic statement of intent. Split equally between East and West Coasters, the LP marks the vinyl debut for many of California's finest, including **Let's Go Bowling** and Skankhead (who soon became **Skankin' Pickle**).

California Ska-Quake happily revisited a few of its predecessor's heroes, but the main focus was on a string of younger acts, winding up with what the rest of the world would regard as the definitive face of California ska circa 1992. It is a fascinating document, and not only in terms of its farsighted delineation of the future of American ska. It also highlighted the dichotomous relationship that existed between the East and West coasts. While the East, or at least Moon's share of it, continued to lean toward the supercharged 2-Tone sound and its own immediate offshoots, the West has never been bound by so readily definable a tradition.

In fact, the early Californian sound evolved not just out of 2-Tone, but also from jazz-based swing, early Jamaican ska, and punk as well. Jump with Joey alone sparked the birth of scores of new groups who would wed jazz to a ska beat. Hepcat took their lead from the Heptones, Toots and the Maytals, and the Paragons. **Operation Ivy** offered adrenaline-spiked skacore; **the Dance Hall Crashers** (led by Op Ivy's Tim Armstrong) lifted heartily from classic '60s pop. What united them was a series of records, singles, and long-players that pushed ska and reggae to the limits of eclecticism without ever delving into the musical obscurity that, perhaps, was the downfall of the British post-punk crew.

Check out Skankin' Pickle's 1994 album ***Sing Along with Skankin' Pickle*** and ask yourself if any album has ever been so aptly titled. And then catch 1995's "My Name Is Erik Yee and My Favorite Band Is Green Day" single. Those seldom-spoken but deeply integral Jamaican attributes of historical respect and musical irreverence are alive and well in the grip of the Pickle.

And still we return to *California Ska-Quake* for one final celebration. Although, when it was first released—and for a couple of years thereafter as well—it would have taken an especially farsighted crystal ball to predict the subsequent superstar status that would engulf one of the bands therein. That band was No Doubt and, to be honest, few people really took them seriously at the time.

They weren't quite a joke, but they were generally dismissed by the ska cognoscenti, and that despite being as true to their roots as any of their better-feted compatriots. Throughout their early club days, No Doubt were firmly wedded to 2-Tone, touting a live set comprised almost exclusively of Specials and Selecter covers. Their one original song was the self-explanatory "No Doubt."

The superstars-to-be development over the ensuing years stands as enduring testament to their senses of self-belief and self-preservation. Although their roots sometimes appeared well-bleached, No Doubt nevertheless paid homage to the past with their 1997 Christmas single, "Oi! To the World," a deliriously ska-ified cover of "Joy to the World."

Before that, however, the band was forced to endure the indignity of effectively being sidelined by their own record label. Signed to Interscope in 1991, their first album underperformed so badly that it would be three years more before they were allowed back onto the release schedule (the band self-released the blistering *The Beacon Street Collection* album during the hiatus).

Once they were back on track, however, there was no stopping them. 1995's ***Tragic Kingdom*** spun off the band's first hit singles, "Just a Girl" and "Spiderwebs," followed by their first monster smash, the utterly un-ska-faced hymnal of "Don't Speak." When another four years passed without new product, it was because the band were too busy touring and promoting the last album.

It would be 2000 before ***The Return of Saturn*** let loose the extraordinarily buoyant "Ex-Girlfriend"; and eighteen months later, *Rock Steady* unleashed the maddeningly compulsive "Hey Baby," pairing them with Jamaican dancehall star Bounty Killer (compatriot Lady Saw and the ubiquitous Sly and Robbie also appear on the album). And while it is true that No Doubt had spiraled a long way from the manic purity of their ska beginnings, it was their embrace of wider Jamaican and American sonics that saw them soar above the rest of the pack to begin with.

Sadly, as so often seems to be the case, No Doubt would not survive their elevation. The media had long grown accustomed to regarding the musicians as simply Stefani's backing band, and the solo career that she launched in 2004 (coinciding with her high-profile marriage to Bush frontman Gavin Rossdale) effectively marked the end of the band. At least until their 2012 return, during which they sounded as joyous and dynamic as ever. Welcome back.

The American ska boom had long since retreated back underground by then; the majors had long since loosened their grip on even the best of the bands they'd once been signing so enthusiastically; and even Moon Ska had been eclipsed, folding in

2000 as sales dropped and the distributors who had once been its lifeblood themselves began to collapse. Bucket would launch a new label, Megalith, to keep the music alive; and every day in some corner of the country, a new ska band emerges to play. You have to hunt for them, though, and maybe that's not such a bad thing. Music always sounds better when it's not served up on a plate.

Unless, of course, it's a dub plate.

We know him best as U-Roy, but other people weren't so certain—even on his own hit singles. (Author's collection)

19

TRIP-HOP: A DEEPER DUB

For years, Horace Andy was one of Jamaica's forgotten talents. Through the early 1970s, he was one of the brightest stars in the entire world of reggae, a young man blessed with a falsetto that would soon be influencing an entire generation of performers. He had been recording ever since, effortlessly turning out a string of gems that built into one of the most magnificent repertoires of the 1970s and early 1980s. But fashions change, new movements emerge, and as Jamaican music braced to embrace the new wave of dancehall, Andy was just one of many who fell precipitously from fashion.

Then in 1991, the British dance act **Massive Attack** scored one of the most spectacular debut hits of the year with their ***Blue Lines*** album, a record that not only ushered in the age of trip-hop and gave meaning to the music of Portishead, **Tricky**, and so many more, but that also introduced—and reintroduced—the world to one of the finest vocal talents of the age: the now-forty-year-old Horace Andy. And with that reintroduction there came a hail of reissues that suddenly transformed Andy into one of the most visible Jamaican stars in the world.

Horace Andy was just sixteen when he cut his first single, "This Is a Black Man's Country" in 1967, but it was 1970 before his career took off, under the aegis of producer Coxsone Dodd. Seldom out of the Jamaican chart over the next few years, Andy scored first with "Got to Be Sure," the self-composed ballad he performed at his audition for Dodd; but it was "Skylarking" in 1973 for which he will be best remembered, a gorgeous ballad that remains as captivating today, when so many other artists have covered it, as it was at the time.

From Studio One, Dodd moved onto Bunny Lee's studio, reveling in the producer's free and easy approach to recording; reveling, too, in his ready embrace of the rootsier material that Andy wanted to record. "You Are My Angel," "Zion Gate," and "Money Money" kept him on the chart; while the sheer majesty of his vocals ensured that he was in constant demand by other artists. In 1975, Andy teamed with DJ Tappa Zukie to write and record "Natty Dread a Weh She Want," while other projects paired him with **Jah Stitch** and Dr. Alimantado. A new version of "Skylarking" brought fresh, darker meaning to the song; Zukie's **"Better Collie"** was correspondingly brightened, without ever losing sight of its maker's intentions; and Marley's "Natural Mystic," one of the last songs Andy recorded before relocating to the United States in 1977, became a more ethereal prayer than even its composer had attempted.

Basing himself in Connecticut, Andy recorded the classic ***In the Light*** album with producer Everton DaSilva (Prince Jammy handled the corresponding ***In the Light Dub***), but further triumphs were cut short when DaSilva was murdered in 1979. Andy continued recording through the 1980s, but declining attention and Jamaican radio's insistence on terming him a golden oldie sent him to London, where he announced his comeback with the at-least-enjoyable ***Seek and You Will Find*** album. That was where Massive Attack found him, sending over the rhythm that he would turn into the hit "One Love," and inaugurating a partnership that still thrives today. And today, no one thinks of Andy as a simple golden oldie.

Indeed, startling though it felt when the partnership was first unveiled, today it is difficult to think of either Andy or Massive Attack without hearing the other; and that despite the British group, too, now boasting a vast catalogue of albums and singles cut with Andy far from the studio, if not necessarily far from their mind.

Massive Attack emerged from the western English city of Bristol, one of those areas that the late 1970s and early 1980s music press liked to describe as a racial melting pot. Local reggae bands like Black Roots, Talisman, and Restriction placed the city's Caribbean community on the map; the predominantly immigrant St. Paul's and Clifton neighborhoods were home to the hottest sound-system shows; and record stores like Revolver were the first port of call for the latest reggae and dub titles, while storeowner Grant Marshall could often be found DJ-ing at the Dug Out in Clifton, catalyzing the scene even further with devastating reggae-dub-funk-punk sets.

It was there that a loose coterie of kids, black and white, coalesced into the Wild Bunch, a DJ posse whose membership reads like a who's who of the later 1980s British club scene: Nellee Hooper, Miles Johnson, Rob Chant and Rob Smith (later to surface as the Smith and Mighty duo), Neneh Cherry, Robert el Naja, and Andrew Vowles, together with sundry former members of the Pop Group and future stars of Rip Rig and Panic. And where many of them came together was on a series of sessions convened by Mark Stewart in 1992.

Stewart told journalist Jo-Ann Greene, "I was in Bristol, and I started to record another album. [And] if it had come out, it would have been the first of what they call[ed] the Bristol Beat. It was a year or two ahead, and a lot of the musicians on it later became Portishead, Tricky, and masses of stuff; that sound continued through those people. But I immediately got bored with it." The projected album was scrapped, but from those sessions, "Tricky was born. I helped him do his first single, made the music, and put him up on his little ladder."

The erstwhile Adrian Thaws had been around the scene since his schooldays, making his live debut at a Smith and Mighty show, toasting to the headliners' reworking of Erik Satie's "Gymnopedie #1." The so-called Tricky Kid began gigging regularly, performing with the Shockwave sound system, at the same time as the now-solidified Massive Attack commenced their rise by accompanying Neneh Cherry on her *Raw Like Sushi* album in 1988. But the new decade would be underway before the Massive trio of 3D, Mushroom, and Daddy G truly showed what they could do.

First up was a brace of singles, "Daydreaming" and "Unfinished Symphony," and then it was on to an album crafted around the sound-system shocks that had fermented their musical vision in the first place, a series of collaborative twists and turns that drew in contributions from Tricky and vocalist Shara Nelson. Also called in was Horace Andy to voice the defining "One Love." The upshot was the almighty *Blue Lines*, which *Goldmine* magazine's Amy Hanson called "an aural tapestry of slick grooves and urban sensibility that took the listener on a journey from dark to light and back again."

Neneh Cherry, meanwhile, had her own new album, *Homebrew*, and new collaborators too. Producer Geoff Barrow's Portishead grew out of the same Coach House studios that had already spawned Massive Attack, and suddenly the media had a new term to bandy about: trip-hop, a seamless fusion of rhythm, dub, atmosphere, and electronics, the ultimate chill-out that could turn savage at any moment.

Portishead's Adrian Utley recalls the fervent energy with which the music of the next few years was created. "From the very first day, there was no concept obviously of what would happen with it, but it was a very exciting feeling for all of us to work together on it. It was done from completely that point of view; it was a new adventure for us, discovering stuff and enjoying doing this, working too hard and loving it, hating it, all the things you do when you make a record. But it had this feeling of new ground to us. I don't think we thought we were being particularly innovative, but we felt good about it."

Massive Attack would buck furiously against their music's pigeonholing (as so often happens, it was the media, not the musicians, who coined the name), taking the most dramatic step when they handed the tapes for their second album, ***Protection***, over to the Mad Professor to manipulate as he saw fit.

Led off by the singles "Sly," "Protection," and "Karmacoma," *Protection* had already re-colored the blue lines of old. The Professor just took things further, emerging with an album that *Goldmine* magazine's Amy Hanson summarized thusly in August 1998: "Dozy dub grooves augmented by smashing loops and big beats ... ***No Protection*** was akin to looking at *Protection* through Alice's looking glass. The Mad Professor didn't so much change the songs as propel them into an alternate dimension. It was a startlingly different take on an already fresh sound."

And still Massive Attack surged forward. In the studio with Horace Andy, they cut a fresh version of "Skylarking" as the title track for a new compilation of his older material. They recorded with Madonna, and scored the movie *187*. If trip-hop fever had not already petered out by the time they reached their third album, 1998's ***Mezzanine***, its deep dislocation and subtle manipulations would have killed it anyway.

The turbulence that always lay at the heart of Massive's journeys through the darkness at the edge of dub was now a ruinous landscape populated by nocturnal electronics, crushing claustrophobia, and phobic imagery (captured well in music but hammered home by the band's best videos). Startling, too, was the sheer symphonic grandiosity of the music's sparseness, the individual tracks hanging alone but blending, too, into one solid whole ... or one dark hole, should you prefer. The sound of one long night spent waiting for a visitor, but never being certain if you want them to arrive. Mashing the Slits' and Dr. Alimantado's late-1970s takes on the same song, Massive Attack's version of "Man Next Door," with Horace Andy offering his most fragile tremulous, tones to the gloom, is worth the price of admission alone.

THE MEN NEXT DOOR

If the Paragons were remembered only for recording the original version of singer John Holt's "Man Next Door" (also known as "A Quiet Place"), they would already be regarded among the Jamaican 1960s' most remarkable talents. But that song was just one of a wealth of stupendous songs that the band recorded throughout their lifespan, while former members Holt and **Bob Andy** would maintain the hit-making traditions once they launched their own solo careers.

Originally recording with Coxsone Dodd, the Paragons kicked off in 1964 with "Good Luck and Goodbye," which turned out to be Andy's first and only major release with the band. He headed off for solo pastures (and later, an internationally renowned duo with **Marcia Griffiths**, Bob and Marcia); the surviving Paragons realigned themselves as a trio and dove headfirst into the fast-percolating rocksteady scene.

A new face for the old calypso classic "Island in the Sun" proved a major success; elsewhere, with Holt's pen and voice at the forefront of all the group did, the Paragons set the bar for harmony groups with a succession of quick-fire gems: "Talking Love," "If I Were You," "Only a Smile," "Mercy Mercy Mercy," "Riding on a High and Windy Day," "The Same Song," "So Depressed," "We Were Meant to Be," "You Mean the World to Me," "Happy Go Lucky Girl," "Love Brings Pain," "On the Beach," and "My Best Girl." There's a killer compilation right there, and the Paragons still hadn't gotten around to making their finest singles.

"Wear You to the Ball Tonight" would become a staple in the young UB40's repertoire in the early 1980s, as well as providing toaster U-Roy with his first major smash in 1969; "The Tide Is High" was an international chart-topper for New York New Wavers Blondie in 1981. And then came "Man Next Door," released as Holt launched a parallel solo career in 1968, and an expression of such dark paranoia and shifting fear that it's hard to believe it is simply a three-minute song. It should be a Hitchcock movie.

Portishead, too, struck one album that—no matter how much you enjoy its successors—can never be surpassed. The sound of midnight on a mid-1970s movie set, torch singers by torchlight, and slow, panning breakbeats, Beth Gibbons and Geoff Barrow had been scheming what became 1994's *Dummy* for over a year before they started recording. Adrian Utley had been composing film scores for longer than that. And that, Utley explains, "is what brought us together. Geoff came in from being a DJ, playing old soundtracks and sampling them, and I came in from always having an interest, and knowing how to write the music, and make the sounds."

Barrow's love of hip-hop swept the soundscapes with a seductive pulse, shattered by Gibbons's haunted corncrake husk even without hearing the myriad remixes that spread "Sour Times" across the emotional spectrum. Her plaintive insistence that "nobody loves me" became one of the musical catchphrases of the early to mid-1990s, a gabba-gabba-hey for the confessional grunge generation.

Elsewhere, "Numb" and the closing "Glory Box" would assert themselves as the foundations upon which a new revolution was being built. Subpoenaed by Tricky (for his "Hell Is Around the Corner," the signature hit on his *Maxinquaye* debut album the following year), and then hijacked by positively anyone else who could spell the words "trip-hop," "Glory Box" in particular remains the summation *not* of all that trip-hop promised during its moments in the commercial sun, but of all that its progenitors would go on to accomplish.

A decade or more later, new albums from Tricky (2008's oft-autobiographical ***Knowle West Boy***), Portishead (*Third*, 2008), and Massive Attack (***Heligoland***, 2010) remain as unique and individual as their makers' earlier efforts. Truly; and no matter what other indignities may have been slung at the trip-hop label in their wake, they were pioneers in a manner that Bob Marley would not have simply recognized, he would also have identified as his own.

The punky reggae party never ends. (Author's collection)

20

PUNK-O-RAMA: THE RANCID STATES OF AMERICA

No matter how highly history now speaks of them, Opera-tion Ivy were never going to break out of their immediate Southern Californian environs. Too tumultuous for mainstream tastes, too closely wedded to the "core" half of the skacore equation, Operation Ivy folded long before ska became a living, breathing force on the American music scene; they had already splintered into new bands by then, and were looking to new directions as well.

Bassist Matt Freeman was touring with the hardcore punks MDC (Millions of Dead Cops), and guitarist Tim Armstrong had more or less abandoned music altogether. By 1991, when Freeman returned from a European tour with the plans for a new band in mind, Armstrong was living and working in a Salvation Army shelter. He went along with his old bandmate's latest idea, because what else was there to do?

With drummer Brett Reed completing the trio (second guitarist Lars Frederiksen joined the following year), Rancid debuted as a straight-ahead hardcore band in late 1991 with a frenetic gig at a friend's post-Christmas party followed by a raw and blistered single for the SoCal-based Lookout label. But those were merely their opening shots. Just as Operation Ivy wedded ska to hardcore, Rancid would marry ska to melodic punk, taking their cue from sources as far apart as the Clash (of course) and British post-punk dance mavens New Order—whose musical emphasis on a signature (and often complex) bass sound dynamically informed the band's burgeoning sound.

Still beholden to the hardcore sound in the studio, it was live that Rancid's musical future would unfurl. Their onstage eye for ska and reggae rhythms was absent from their debut; and it would merely be hinted at on their second album, ***Let's Go***. But it was reinforced by the energetic "I Wanna Riot" on the *Punk-O-Rama* compilation album; and it blasted into tumultuously Day-Glo prominence across their third album, the landmark ***...And Out Come the Wolves***.

Freeman told *Goldmine* magazine's Jo-Ann Greene about the delay. "That's the big debate, I suppose. Even with the first record, people were like, 'Why don't you play any ska?' You know, we could have come out with a fucking record that sounded exactly like Operation Ivy, and it probably would've sold a lot more, but at the time, that's not what we were feeling. We wanted to do a hard fucking record, and that's what we did. The second record was what we felt, too, and it just came along, but we dabbled in ska all the way through.

"If you listen to *Let's Go*, you can hear some ska lines. There's a lot in there; it's all over the fucking place. Look at 'As One'; there you go, right there. It's always going to be there; look at the bass lines I'm playing. Even on the first record, there's a lot of ska-based type of things. That influence is going to come out, it just sort of first reared its head on . . . *Wolves* for whatever reason, but I think it's been a building thing for a long time."

"Time Bomb," the album's first single, led the way, a pounding ska rocker that eased the listener into two further skankers, "Daly City Train" and "Old Friend," to complete a triptych of astonishing blasts that truly positioned the band alongside their idols, the Clash. A mood that "Ruby Soho," a true Clash City Rocker if ever there was one, only accentuated. In 2012, Jimmy Cliff would take "Ruby Soho" for his own, and maybe paint the song in the colors that Rancid might themselves have had in mind when they first recorded it. But if anybody still doubted the group's credentials, Cliff's revival sent them packing.

And of course it was only the beginning. The band's next album, 1998's *Life Won't Wait*, saw the Rancid sound expand almost beyond recognition.

They toyed with a remarkable rocksteady hybrid across "Cocktails," then swung into the calypso-beaten "Coppers" (featuring ska vocalist **Dr. Israel** and Jane's Addiction drummer Stephen Perkins on steel drums!). The title track, one of two songs recorded in Jamaica (the other was "Hoover Street") roped in Buju Banton to co-write and perform on a wild blast of dancehall punk, while other guest appearances included bows from No Doubt's Eric Stefani, the Bosstones' Dicky Barrett, Hepcat's Greg Lee, and sundry Specials and **Slackers**.

By now, Tim Armstrong was also operating his own record label, Hellcat (Rancid's next album, 2000's eponymous set, would be their first for the imprint), taking off just as Moon Ska began to sink and picking up their baton with glee. Hepcat, **the Pietasters**, and **the Gadjits** were among Hellcat's earliest signings, **the Dropkick Murphys** and Joe Strummer among its most successful, and the Slackers among its longest lived.

The Slackers had been playing around the New York club circuit since the mid-1980s. Originally, and unsurprisingly, they were most heavily influenced by 2-Tone. That all changed, however, with the 1994 arrival of former Hepcat tenor saxophonist Dave Hillyard and ex-Allstonians trumpeter Jeremy Mushlin. Both were firmly embedded in a far wider-ranging musical stew than the rest of their bandmates, and the ensuing change was extraordinary; compare the Slackers' "Sister Sister," on 1994's ***Skarmageddon*** compilation, to anything on their debut LP ***Better Late Than Never***. Leaving the checkerboard world of 2-Tone behind, the Slackers now became true to their name, with a true slack, rocksteady sound mixed with jazz-tinged horn solos, reggae beats, and traditional ska. A nonstop dance party whose magic was effortlessly translated onto the band's exquisite second album, ***Redlight***.

Since that time ...the Slackers' *nineteenth* album, ***The Great Rocksteady Swindle***, was released in 2010, and it caught the band still as gloriously frenzied as ever—a way of life that frontman Vic Ruggiero encapsulates with the words that welcome every visitor to theslackers.com:

"The Slackers are part of an imaginary universe. It wasn't their fault—well, not completely. The caterpillar told them not to eat the mushroom on the right. But they did; and for fifteen years now, they've had to play Imaginary-Jamaican-Rock-and-Roll, and try to explain that to everyone who passes. One asks, 'Are you a reggae band? Where are your dreadlocks, then?' Another says, '*You don't sound like punk rock with horns at all!*' One elderly gent says, 'Why, it sounds like a lot of music I used to like, but I don't think any of you boys look addicted to *heroin!*'"

It's a hard life, to be sure.

But, ska, rocksteady, reggae, roots, *nyahbinghi*, dancehall, call it what you will, if you like Bob Marley (and if you've read this far, you must), it doesn't matter what name the music labors beneath this week, or what an audience might expect of it. It forever moves outward, and it forever soars upward and onward, forever evolving, forever changing, forever finding new mediums to mate with.

Maybe it is all a long way from the primitive purity of ye olden days; from the righteous dread of the mid-1970s, or from whatever other golden era your own ears will automatically gravitate towards. But that is what makes the music so important today, the fact that it has learned to step beyond its own immediate strictures and joyfully embrace its neighbors ... the man next door, indeed.

But what is even more important is the fact that it will continue to do so, long after any current media fascination has abated, and the facile fashion-spotters have found other trends to trail behind. None of that really matters, after all, because just like Prince Buster said, just like Madness said, and just like the events of the past fifty years have proven, reggae music will always travel at the head of the pack. It will always be one step beyond.

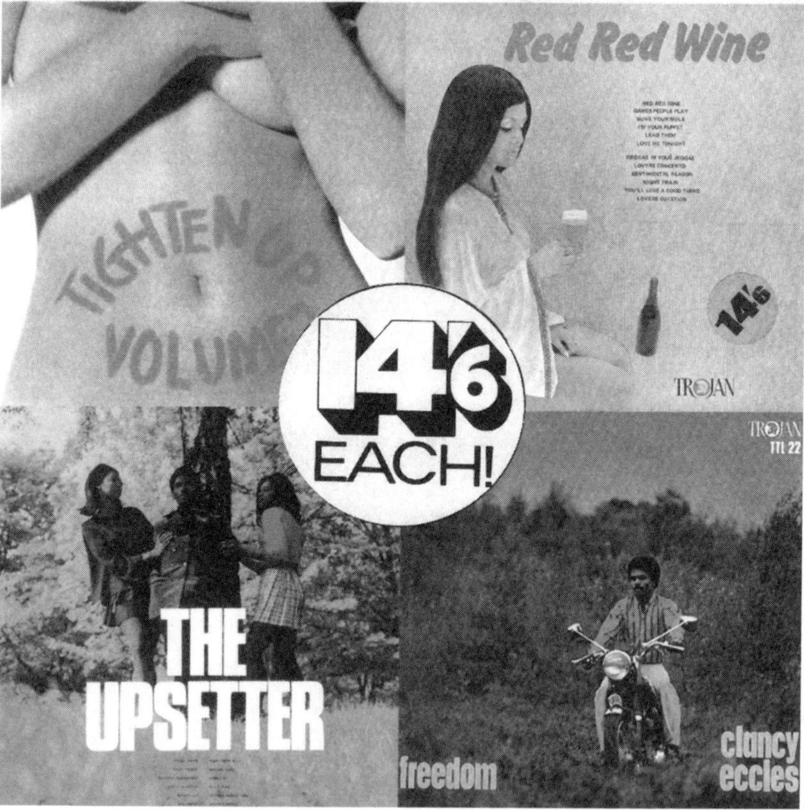

Four classic albums, four classic jackets. (Author's collection)

21

FINALLY, FORTY FURTHER FABULOUS MARLEY COVERS

"AFRICA UNITE"—FRESHLYGROUND (2010)

Marley's later albums offered slim pickings for would-be covers, but the South African Afropoppers Freshlyground did a fine job with "Africa Unite."

"AFRICAN HERBSMAN"—ZIGGY MARLEY AND THE MELODY MAKERS (1993)

Yes, it's a cover, but Marley Sr.'s lyric made it his own. Junior just holds it even closer.

"BEND DOWN LOW"—GREGORY ISAACS (1975)

Recorded during the Cool Ruler's time with producer Sidney Crooks, "Bend Down Low" is more a showcase for Isaacs's voice than for the song. And that should be recommendation enough.

"BUFFALO SOLDIER"—MAFIA AND FLUXY (1999)

One of the crucial rhythm sections of the 1990s and beyond, the British team of Mafia and Fluxy released ***Soul of the Gong*** in 1999, and gifted us with one of the finest of all Marley tribute collections. Two CDs' worth of material include some truly primal dubs.

"CHANCES ARE"—THE BREEDERS (2009)

Formed from the wreckage of late 1980s indie rockers the Pixies, Kim Deal's Breeders cut this shimmering acoustic take with producer Steve Albini. Included on the EP *Fate to Fatal.*

"CONCRETE JUNGLE"—DENNIS BROWN (1993)

There was a fabulous version of this cut by King Sporty in Miami around 1974, with KC and the Sunshine Band providing backup, and a girlie backing chorus who actually do go "ha ha ha, ha ha ha" after the line about laughing like a clown.

But in case that's *not* the way (uh-huh uh-huh) you like it, "Concrete Jungle" turns up on the Lloyd Chambers–produced ***The General***; not one of Brown's most indispensable albums, but certainly one of the best of his later releases.

"COULD YOU BE LOVED"—JOE COCKER (1997)

A remarkable recording pushes the original reggae-lite ballad into almost hard-rock territory. Having been one of the first white Englishmen to work with Sly and Robbie back in the early 1980s, Joe Cocker was no stranger to reggae by the time he recorded this (for 1997's *Across from Midnight* album); the ease with which he translated it to his more traditional milieu, then, only adds to the performance's power.

"CRAVEN CHOKE PUPPY"—BIG YOUTH (1975)

A stunning revision of the Marley original, instantly recognizable but utterly unique, too.

"CRAZY BALDHEAD"—JOHNNY CLARKE (1976)

Clarke had already been making waves around the Kingston scene by the time he hooked up with Bunny Lee in 1975, but still nobody could have predicted the sheer brilliance that he was about to unleash.

Kicking off with the fiery roots of the ***None Shall Escape the Judgement*** album, Lee and team maintained a stream of essential singles and albums ranging from further militancy via "Cold I Up," "Enter into His Gates with Praise," and "Joshua's Word"; some excellent lovers rock; and a stream of spot-on covers. Clarke's version of the Wailers' "No Woman, No Cry" sold more than 40,000 copies in Jamaica alone. 1976's ***Authorized Version*** hosts his take on "Crazy Baldhead," and it is just one of so many highlights.

"DO IT TWICE"—SISTAH ROBI KAHAKALAU (2006)

A gorgeous rendition by Hawaii's Sistah Robi.

"DON'T ROCK MY BOAT"—MAX ROMEO (1976)

A Bunny Lee production, recorded in those manic months leading up to Romeo's pairing with Lee Perry for *War ina Babylon.* So much of Romeo's output is worth hearing, particularly once he moved into the early to mid-1970s, but his work with Lee surpasses most.

"DUPPY CONQUEROR"—THE GLADIATORS (1980)

A cut from **the Gladiators**' eponymous album, their last (and weakest) for the Front Line label, and one of the few cuts therein that harkens back to the true power of the group; the ***Trenchtown Mix Up*** and ***Proverbial Reggae*** albums are the real place to start.

"EASY SKANKING"—JOHNNY CLARKE (1979)

Yes, it's Johnny again.

"GET UP, STAND UP"—BIG YOUTH (1976)

Bob Marley and Peter Tosh's international rabble-rouser, pushed into even more virulent quarters by the always-phenomenal Big Youth.

"GUAVA JELLY"—JOHNNY NASH (1972)

American singer Johnny Nash was visiting Jamaica and attending a Rastafarian grounation when he met the Wailers in 1968, igniting an on-again, off-again partnership that would culminate in Marley's first major international hit.

Nash had already recorded a rocksteady-flavored album, ***Hold Me Tight***; Marley's influence would inescapably influence Nash's future work, while the Wailers were repaid with a handful of recording sessions overseen by Nash and his business partner. A single credited to **Bob, Rita and Peter**, "Bend Down Low," was released in the U.S. soon after, while other material would begin to leak out on a variety of labels following Marley's death.

Nash visited Sweden in 1971 to score the movie *Love Is Not a Game*. Marley accompanied him, remaining by Nash's side for a Swedish tour and then heading to London where the rest of the band joined him. There, work began on Nash's next album, together with a handful more Wailers recordings; these, too, have dribbled out over the years. But Nash's album was an immediate smash; ***I Can See Clearly Now*** included four Marley songs: "Comma Comma," "Guava Jelly," "You Poured Sugar on Me" (co-written with Nash), and "Stir It Up," a flute-led mock-rock steady romp that topped the chart in the U.S. and made #5 in Britain.

"HYPOCRITE"—THE SPECIAL BEAT (1990)

The Special Beat grew, as their name suggests, from the remains of two of the key bands from the U.K. ska revival a decade earlier, the Specials and the Beat...or the English Beat, as they were referred to in America.

Of the two, the Specials were the social commentators; the Beat, while not shying away from politics, were more generally regarded simply as the purveyors of a tough, danceable sound. And while they quickly skanked far from the 2-Tone pigeonhole that devoured so many other bands of their ilk and age, they were certainly pursuing similar demons as they rose out of hometown Birmingham in 1979 with a ska-punk collision that matched social politics with sociological awareness—then turned the whole thing into a nonstop dance party.

They were promptly rewarded with the first of thirteen U.K. hit singles scored over the next four years, but more surprising was the band's American breakthrough, where they outperformed both the period figureheads of the Specials and Madness, and ultimately hauled themselves into that rarefied, if grotesquely uninformed strata where they came to epitomize "ska" in the same way that UB40 represented "reggae." It didn't matter that purists would run a mile at the thought of such a comparison. No one ever went Top 40 by appealing to purists.

"Tears of a Clown," "Hands Off She's Mine," "Mirror in the Bathroom," "Stand Down Margaret," "Too Nice to Talk To," "Save It for Later," and more offered up a litany of lean rhythms, sonic ska, and, for anyone with even half an ear for great dance music, an irrepressible legend. Later in life, too, the somewhat irritating "I Confess" and a smart cover of Andy Williams's "Can't Get Used to Losing You" highlight just how masterfully the English Beat subverted radio-friendly pop to their own ends.

This was the legacy that the Special Beat clung onto. Reconvening in 1990 for the demo album that spawned "Hypocrite," they proved their versatility had not departed. Other tracks on the tape included Delroy Wilson's "Better Must Come," Prince Buster's "Time Longer Than Rope" (later rerecorded by the band for full release), David Bowie's "Golden Years," and Mitch Ryder's "Breakout."

"I SHOT THE SHERIFF"—EUMIR DEODATO (1976)

Brazilian jazzman Deodato is probably best remembered for his international hit version of "Also Sprach Zarathustra." This is one of his lesser-known efforts, then, buried away on 1976's *Very Together* album, but the fact that it works so well says much for the sheer internationality of Marley's best songwriting.

"I'M STILL WAITING"—DELROY WILSON (1976)

Until his death in 1995, Wilson ranked among of Jamaica's most eternal performers, a hardworking man who cut his first single at age thirteen, and was still going strong up until the end. "Better Must Come" is probably his best-known number—but this Wailers cover, produced by Lloyd Charmers, became one of his biggest hits.

"IRON LION ZION"—MISCONDUCT (2003)

A frenetic assault by the Swedish hardcore punks from their EP *A New Beginning*.

"IS THIS LOVE"—RIHANNA (2008)

The erstwhile Robyn Rihanna Fenty turned in some phenomenal versions during her 2008 tour—check YouTube for details.

"JOHNNY WAS"—STIFF LITTLE FINGERS (1980)

Belfast punks Stiff Little Fingers were among the most militant of British punk bands, a consequence of their upbringing amid the troubles of Northern Ireland. Original compositions "Suspect Device" and "Alternative Ulster" set out the band's agenda very early on; and no matter that "Johnny Was" was written for a situation an ocean away, Stiff Little Fingers' ragged reggae attack rendered it pertinent regardless.

"KAYA"—RONNIE DAVIS (1978)

Recorded almost immediately after the Wailers' own version (on the album of the same name) hit the streets, former Itals frontman Davis turns in a performance that actually rivals the original for atmosphere.

"MELLOW MOOD"—BUNNY WAILER (1981)

One more breathless Bunny performance. You need to hear it!

"MR. CHATTERBOX"—JOHNNY CLARKE (1976)

The Wailers recorded their original version of "Mr. Chatterbox" under the title "Mr. Talkative," then reprised it during their stint with Bunny Lee in the early 1970s. Clarke and Lee then revisited it again; and, while there's no indication as to whom they aimed it (the Wailers pointedly dedicated their take to the garrulous Niney Holness), still Clarke sounds as though he means every word.

"NO WOMAN, NO CRY"—THE FUGEES (1996)

Marley's most oft-covered song has drawn interpretations from across the musical spectrum, but it was Wyclef Jean and the Fugees who truly returned it to the musical map as the penultimate cut on their monster *The Score* album. Solo, the Haitian-born Jean has maintained a firm grasp on roots, even when following other musical notions entirely. But this is the sound of his love affair with the music at its purest.

"PUT IT ON"—I-ROY (1978)

The one track featured on the mighty I-Roy's *Ten Commandments* album that was not culled from *Exodus*. Revised as "Commandment One," it is a thunderous celebration of toasting that nevertheless retains the spirit of the original song.

"RAINBOW COUNTRY"—DENNIS BROWN (1996)

Another late-in-the-day Brown epic, recorded with producer Musclehead within a string of singles that included the effervescent "Keep It Up," "Feeling the Spirit," and "Rocky Love," together with the album *You Got the Best of Me*.

"RASTAMAN CHANT"—RAS MICHAEL AND THE SONS OF NEGUS (1974)

The crown princes of *nyahbinghi*, Ras Michael and the Sons of Negus were a Rastafarian commune whose meetings were a magnet for many musicians in the early 1960s, the Wailers among them. Michael was also the host of Jamaican radio's first-ever Rasta-themed program, *The Lion of Judah Time*, in 1966 (the show also titled the group's first single the following year); while the band's "Ethiopian National Anthem" was co-opted by Peter Tosh and U-Roy for the intro to their "(Earth's) Rightful Ruler" single. "Rastaman Chant," the Wailers' own most potent nod in the direction of *nyahbinghi*, was certainly cut under the influence of the Sons of Negus; it only made sense, then, that the Sons should swiftly take it back.

"RAT RACE"—MAFIA AND FLUXY (1999)

See "Buffalo Soldier."

"REBEL MUSIC (3 O'CLOCK ROADBLOCK)" —JACOB MILLER AND THE INNER CIRCLE (1975)

Inner Circle, fronted by the larger-than-life Miller, were among the bands that arose from the roots explosion and, for a time in the late 1970s, seriously threatened the Wailers' supremacy. The two bands co-headlined the legendary Peace Festival, and had Miller not perished in an auto accident in 1980, Inner Circle might well have rivaled Black Uhuru for Marley's crown.

"Rebel Music" dates from Miller's early years with the already-established Inner Circle, and a clutch of sessions that also included reggaefied takes on such American soul hits as "Rock the Boat," "TSOP," "When Will I See You Again," "You Make Me Feel Brand New," and a remarkable adaptation of Rupie Edwards's "Ire Feelings," completely stripped of its original dub tones.

IF YOU LIKE "REDEMPTION SONG" . . .

It was one of those juxtapositions that cultural legend is defined by, the placing of "Redemption Song" as the final track on the final album Bob Marley would ever record.

Uprising was not, compared to all that had gone before, Marley and the Wailers' strongest album. Indeed, reviews that circulated around its original release were less than complimentary, with even the signature hit "Could You Be Loved" being little more than a typical slice of Marley-style lovers rock, and other tracks (most notably "Pimper's Paradise" and "Work," simply sounding unfinished).

But then the needle touched "Redemption Song," another song that could possibly have benefitted from a little more time, and suddenly all was forgiven. For the sparseness, the tremulous vocal, the scarred lament all worked here. Months before Marley died, before the awful truth of his final illness became common knowledge, there was something about "Redemption Song" that seemed to be saying goodbye. And today, it is rightly regarded among Marley's most glorious accomplishments, not only within his own recorded canon, but among the myriad other artists who have recorded it.

Joe Strummer (2003)

The voice of the Clash until their mid-1980s dissolution, Strummer's solo career rarely attained the same musical heights as his old band. But in terms of good will and good-natured rock 'n' reggae roll, the music he recorded alone, with the Latin Rockabilly War and, best of all, the Mescaleros, stands proud regardless.

Never one to acknowledge his own limitations—and forever aware that his own political and cultural convictions were as powerful as any other weapon in his arsenal—Strummer effortlessly followed the Clash's old excursions into reggae with some remarkable performances of his own. He teamed with the **Long Beach Dub Allstars** for a cracked and weary cover of "The Harder They Come"; joined Jimmy Cliff for the lovely "Over the Border"; and then turned out a succession of highlights across three albums recorded over the last few years of his life: 1999's ***Rock Art and the X-Ray Style***, 2001's ***Global a Go-Go***, and ***Streetcore***, posthumously released in 2003 following his death the previous December.

It is there that Strummer's impassioned take on "Redemption Song" can be found; the original pained but defiant version, that is, not the faintly distasteful reinvention that producer Rick Rubin constructed by splicing Strummer's version to Johnny Cash's attempt at the song. Following Strummer's death, "Redemption Song" would take on the same meaning among his fans as it does among Marley's; it titles author Chris Salewicz's 2006 biography of the singer, and it haunts director Julian Temple's *The Future Is Unwritten* documentary.

Jackson Browne (2005)

Once the epitome of the laid-back West Coast singer-songwriter movement, Browne has since developed into one of the elder statesmen of American song. His beautiful acoustic version of "Redemption Song" opened the 2005 Rock and Roll Hall of Fame ceremonies.

Superblue (1993)

Soca star Superblue included a suitably rearranged "Redemption Song" on his *Bacchanal Party* album, the follow-up to the massive "Bacchanal Time" hit single.

Stevie Wonder (1996)

Back in 1980, Stevie Wonder acknowledged his love of Bob Marley with "Master Blaster (Jammin')," a stupendous hit single that celebrated not only a personal friendship, but also a working relationship—Marley and Wonder played a number of live shows together during 1979–1980. In 1996, Wonder returned to the same inspiration for a tender "Redemption Song," recorded for his latest best-of collection, *Song Review—Greatest Hits*.

Manfred Mann's Earth Band (1983)

The first rock cover of the song was the work of the latest incarnation of a band whose musical origins dated back as far as the Wailers; Manfred Mann were one of the original British Invaders in the early 1960s, although they had undergone manifold changes since then. Best remembered now for such defining '70s hits as "Blinded by the Light" and "Davy's on the Road Again," the Earth Band were enjoying something of a revival in the early 1980s, and *Somewhere in Afrika* was rewarded accordingly. "Redemption Song" appears on side two, at the conclusion of the landmark "Africa Suite," and draws a remarkable vocal from frontman Chris Thompson.

Bunny Wailer (1990)

An inevitable inclusion on the *Time Will Tell* Marley tribute album.

Rihanna (2010)

Recorded by the Barbados-born Rihanna as a fundraiser following the earthquake that devastated Haiti in early 2010.

The Chieftains (2002)

Irish folkies the Chieftains have never been afraid to step far outside their own musical milieu, joining with Ziggy Marley in 2002 to record a gloriously hybrid version of the song, a highlight of their album *The Wide World Over: A 40 Year Celebration*.

Sinead O'Connor (1997)

In strict contrast to her take on "War" (see the end of this chapter), O'Connor's equally lovely "Redemption Song" is among her more obscure offerings, an-in concert favorite in 1996 that would be released only as the B-side to her "This Is a Rebel Song" single the following year.

Bob Marley and the Wailers (1980)

Not really a cover, but the bonus tracks included on the remastered *Uprising* included a previously unheard version of "Redemption Song," recorded with the full Wailers band, and setting up a fascinating contrast with the familiar album version.

"ROOTS ROCK REGGAE"—DEAN FRASER (1994)

Jamaican sax supremo Fraser lets loose on another Marley classic, the closing cut from the *Dean Plays Bob* tribute album.

"SMALL AXE"—ALEX HARVEY (1978)

Scottish rocker Harvey had already broken up his Sensational Alex Harvey Band when he came to cut this Marley number for a single in 1978. Reduced to a loose reggae-based shuffle with Harvey's so-distinctive voice spitting out the lyrics, the song was also Harvey's contribution to the massive Rock Against Racism festival at London's Alexandra Palace in 1979.

"SO JAH SEH"—JACKIE EDWARDS (1981)

Edwards was one of the originators of ska, and one of the first Jamaican artists to truly make an impression overseas. An early signing to the newly born Island label, Edwards relocated to the U.K. and wrote several hits for the teenaged Steve Winwood's Spencer Davis Group. Although true international recognition eluded the sweet-voiced songwriter, his career never flagged, and this 1981 single is as electrifying as any of his better-known releases.

"SOUL REBEL"—UB40 (1998)

British band UB40 have packed in a lot of covers around their own reggae-tinged originals, with three separate volumes of *Labour of Love* allowing them to examine their roots in deeper and greater depth. The title cut from the Wailers' Lee Perry–produced album made it onto volume three, and the only question left to answer was: What took them so long? It's great.

"STIR IT UP"—JOHNNY NASH (1972)

See "Guava Jelly."

"THE SUN IS SHINING"—BLACK UHURU (1977)

This was the follow-up to Uhuru's hit version of Marley's "Natural Mystic." "The Sun Is Shining" was recorded with JoJo Hookim at Channel One shortly after the arrival of frontman Michael Rose. Like so much of the group's early work, it is a far cry from the shattered roots of their Island label material, but the promise is already there.

"TALKIN' BLUES"—THE MAROONS (1975)

The Maroons were actually **the Cimarons**, a long-running British reggae band whose cover of "Talkin' Blues" went onto become the first British reggae record ever to top the Jamaican chart. It was also, apparently, a firm favorite of Marley himself.

"THREE LITTLE BIRDS"—KEITH FRANK (2000)

Squeezed out of our *Exodus* roundup a few chapters back, zydeco hero Frank medleys the Marley composition with a gospel number called "No Need to Worry." The ensuing merriment not only highlights that music's influence on Marley's most spiritual compositions, but he does it with an accordion. From the aptly titled album *Ready or Not*.

"TRENCHTOWN ROCK"—SUBLIME (1996)

From their self-titled 1996 album, their first for a major label (and third overall), the long-running Long Beach punks hit the ground running with a ferocious rocker. Alongside the equally dynamic Rancid, Offspring, and Bad Religion, Sublime were perhaps the hardest hitting of all the pioneers whose punky reggae hybrid would epitomize the best of southern California's 1990s scene. Their 1992 debut album, *40oz. to Freedom*, featured covers of "54-46, That's My Number" and "Rivers of Babylon"; *Robbin' the Hood* two years later included Peter Tosh's "Steppin' Razor."

Following the death of frontman Bradley Nowell, also in 1996, the band regrouped as the Long Beach Dub Allstars. They reformed as Sublime in 2009.

"WAR"—SINEAD O'CONNOR (1992)

One of the most important singers of the 1990s and beyond, and one of the most controversial too, Irish-born Sinead O'Connor first came to international prominence via her hit cover of Prince's "Nothing Compares 2 U." It proved a deceptive introduction to one of the most volatile and militant vocalists of her generation, a fiercely political performer who was nevertheless capable of exquisite beauty.

O'Connor's best known visit to the Marley songbook is her a cappella rendition of "War," performed on television's *Saturday Night Live* in 1992, and climaxed by her ripping in half a photograph of the Pope. Still a spectacular piece of television, it is regrettable only that the media firestorm of condemnation that followed so completely obscured the sheer poise and elegance of her performance.

The *SNL* version of "War" remained unreleased until the show was celebrated with a multi-DVD box set, *25 Years of Music Performances and Sketches*, in 1999. Six years later, a studio version of "War" closed out O'Connor's ***Throw Down Your Arms*** album, a collection of twelve reggae covers (plus phenomenal dub versions). Opening with a crystalline (and all-but-unaccompanied) "Jah No Dead" (one of five Burning Spear numbers included within), the set went onto visit the canons of Junior Byles (a breathlessly breathy "Curly Locks"), **Little Roy**, Buju Banton,

Israel Vibration, **Devon Irons** (the oft-overlooked "Vampire"), the Abyssinians, Johnny Clarke, and Peter Tosh ("Down Presser").

ACKNOWLEDGMENTS

Thanks to the usual cast of characters, suspects, and fictional beings for their assistance, advice, and enthusiasm as this book came to life, including: Amy Hanson, Oliver, Toby and Trevor, Jen, Karen and Todd, Linda and Larry, Deb and Roger, Gaye and Tim, Dave and Sue, Bateerz and family, sundry gremlins, Barb East, Geoff Monmouth, and many more.

To Jo-Ann Greene, for permission to quote from her Rancid interviews; and to Ari Up, T. V. Smith, Brian Jobson, Adrian Utley, Roddy Radiation, Neville Staples, Dave Ruffy, Vince Seggs, Joe Strummer, Dennis Bovell, Budgie, and Dicky Barrett, for sharing their memories of the music.

To my editor, Mike Edison; to my copyeditor, Ross Plotkin; to my project editor, Jessica Burr; and to all at Backbeat.

And to the myriad other souls who joined me on this journey, whether to talk, listen, or just pump up the volume …

APPENDIX A: TWO SEVENS CLASHING: 150 ESSENTIAL ROOTS ROCKERS, 1976–1977

1. "A You Me Love"—Dillinger (Stars and Stripes)
2. "African Roots"—Johnny Clarke (Ja-Man)
3. "After Tonight"—Matumbi (Safari)
4. "Angola"—The Revolutionaries (Disco Mix)
5. "Babylon Bawling"—Lambert Douglas (Rosso)
6. "Babylon Burning"—L.A.B. (Love)
7. "Babylon Kingdom Fall"—Prince George (Stud)
8. "Babylon Queendom"—Peter Tosh (Intel Diplo)
9. "Babylon Too Rough"—Gregory Isaacs (Belmont)
10. "Babylon Trap Them"—Danny Clarke and Dobson's Disciples (Wild Flower)
11. "Back to Africa"—Aswad (Island)
12. "Ballistic Affair"—Leroy Smart (Well Charge)
13. "The Barber Feel It"—Dr. Alimantado and Jah Stitch (Jackpot)
14. "Bionic Dread"—Dillinger (Black Swan)
15. "Black a Kill Black"—Gregory Isaacs (African Museum)
16. "Bosrah"—Ras Allah (Kiss)
17. "Bring It On Home to Me"—Johnny Clarke (Caribbean)
18. "Bump and Skank"—Dillinger (Love)
19. "Bur-O-Boy"—Junior Byles (Ethnic Fight)
20. "Can You Feel It"—Junior Byles (Thing)
21. "Cave Man Skank"—Ranking Trevor (Disco Mix)
22. "Chain Gang"—Matumbi (Matumbi)
23. "Chant Down Babylon"—Junior Byles (Black Wax)
24. "Chase the Devil"—Max Romeo (Island)

25. "Counter Attack"—Revolutionaries (Channel One)
26. "Country Style"—Dillinger (Jay Wax)
27. "Crazy Baldhead"—Johnny Clarke (Justice)
28. "Danger Zone"—Jah Stitch (Locks)
29. "Daughter of Zion"—Bagga (Matumbi)
30. "Disgraceful Woman"—Johnny Clarke (Attack)
31. "Diverse Doctrine"—Ras Ibuna (Pittsburgh)
32. "Don't Call Us Immigrants"—Tabby "Cat" Kelly (Tank)
33. "Dreadlocks Party"—Little Joe (Belmont)
34. "Dreamland"—Bunny Wailer (Island)
35. "East Man Skank"—Dillinger (Well Charge)
36. "Exodus"—Bob Marley and the Wailers (Island)
37. "False Teaching"—Junior Murvin (Well Charge)
38. "Fight I Down"—Lizzard (Belmont)
39. "Flat Foot Hustling"—Dillinger (Observer)
40. "Free Black People"—Burning Spear (Total Sounds)
41. "Gimme Me Gun"—Dr. Alimantado (Ital)
42. "Groovy Situation"—Keith Rowe (Upsetter)
43. "Gypsy Woman"—Milton Henry (Cactus)
44. "Hang On Sloopy"—Trinity (Well Charge)
45. "Have Mercy"—The Mighty Diamonds (Virgin)
46. "Heavy Manners"—Prince Far I (Heavy Duty)
47. "Here I Come"—Dennis Brown (Observer)
48. "His Majesty"—The In Crowd (Cactus)
49. "His Majesty Is Coming"—The In Crowd (Evolution)
50. "Hit the Road Jack"—Big Youth (Trojan)
51. "I and I Can't Turn Back"—Mickey Simpson (Total Sound)
52. "I'm Alright"—Jah Woosh (Attack)
53. "I'm Still in Love with You"—Marcia Aitken (Belmont)
54. "Immanuelle God Is Coming"—Dennis Brown (DEB)
55. "It Was Love"—Brent Dowe (Student)
56. "Ital Dish"—I-Roy (Sunshot)
57. "Jah Bring I Joy"—Bobby Melody (Trojan)
58. "Jah Forgive Them"—Leroy Smart (Micron)
59. "Jah Jah Bring Everything"—Jah Glenn (Eagle)
60. "Jah Jah Go Beat Them"—Cornell Campbell (Jackpot)

61. "Jah Will Guide"—Silver Shadows (Well Charge)
62. "Johnny Was"—Bob Marley and the Wailers (Island)
63. "Judas the White Belly Rat"—Lee Perry (Upsetters)
64. "Judgement on the Land"—The Prophets (Prophet)
65. "Kingston 11"—Royal Rasses (God Sent)
66. "Leftist"—Revolutionaries (Disco Mix)
67. "Legalise It"—Peter Tosh (Virgin)
68. "Let It Be Me"—Honeyboy and Winston Curtis (Jamatel)
69. "Let's Get Started"—Tetrack (Rockers)
70. "Love Jah and Live"—Jah Woosh (Kiss)
71. "Love Jah Jah Children"—Big Youth (Chanon Jah)
72. "Man in Me"—Matumbi (Matumbi)
73. "Mango Walk"—The Crowd (Tropical Sound Tracs)
74. "Money"—Delroy Wilson (Morwells)
75. "MPLA"—The Revolutionaries (Disco Mix)
76. "MPLA"—Tappa Zukie (Klik)
77. "My Time"—Dennis Brown (Morpheus)
78. "Native Land"—I-Roy (Thing)
79. "Natty B.Sc."—Dillinger (Black Swan)
80. "Natty Don't Make War"—Little Joe (Melrose)
81. "Natty Kung Fu"—Dillinger (Forward)
82. "Natty Pass Through Rome"—Prince Jazzbo (Black Art)
83. "Natty Sing a Hit Song"—Dillinger (Arab)
84. "No Mans Land"—Cornell Campbell (Joe Gibbs)
85. "On a Saturday Night"—Christine (Observer)
86. "One Step Forward"—Max Romeo (Island)
87. "Party Time"—Heptone (Island)
88. "Philistines on the Land"—Junior Murvin (Upsetter)
89. "Pichy Pachy"—Junior Byles (Ja-Man)
90. "Pickney Have Pickney"—Well Pleased and Satisfied (High Note)
91. "Police and Thieves"—Junior Murvin (Island)
92. "Pressure inna Babylon"—Dennis Alcapone (Ethnic Fight)
93. "Pride and Ambition"—Leroy Smart (Channel One EP)
94. "Punky Reggae Party"—Bob Marley and the Wailers
95. "Ragnampiza"—Dillinger (Well Charge)

96. "Rasta Business"—Gregory Isaacs (Olympic)
97. "Riverboat"—Big Youth (Negusa Negast)
98. "Rock to Sleep"—Horace Andy (International)
99. "Rockers"—Tappa Zukie (Klik)
100. "Rockers No Crackers"—Glen Washington (Student)
101. "Roots Music"—Jackie Bernard (Grounation)
102. "Roots Rock Reggae"—Bob Marley and the Wailers (Island)
103. "Roots Train Number 1"—Junior Murvin (Black Art)
104. "Runaway Girl"—U-Roy (Virgin)
105. "Satta I"—Lizzard (Black Wax)
106. "Satta in the Place"—Big Joe (Micron)
107. "Self Defence"—Dr. Alimantado (Ital)
108. "Set the Captives Free"—Gregory Isaacs (DEB)
109. "Shark Out Deh"—Errol Holt (Ja-Man)
110. "Shine Eye Gal"—Black Uhuru (Taxi)
111. "Six Dead and Nineteen Gone to Jail"—Big Youth (Observer)
112. "Slave Master"—Gregory Isaacs (Thing)
113. "Smile Jamaica"—Bob Marley and the Wailers (Tuff Gong)
114. "Soldier and Police War"—Jah Lion (Island)
115. "South Africa"—Mighty Travellers (Travellers)
116. "Speak and Say"—Big Joe (Soul Beat)
117. "Spear Burning"—Burning Spear (Spear)
118. "Special Request"—Dennis Alcapone (Jackpot)
119. "State of Emergency"—Joe Gibbs and the Professionals (Joe Gibbs)
120. "Step on the Dragon"—I-Roy (Observer)
121. "Sticks Man"—Black Slate (Slate)
122. "Stop the War in Babylon"—James Brown (Mango)
123. "Sufferers Time"—Heptones (Black Art)
124. "Ten Against One"—Big Youth (Negusa Negast)
125. "Ten Against One"—Tappa Zukie (Klik)
126. "Tenement Yard"—Jacob Miller (Grounation)
127. "Things and Time"—Wailing Souls (Well Charge)
128. "Three Babylon"—Aswad (Island)
129. "Three Black People"—Burning Spear (Island)
130. "Three Pan One a Murder"—Rupie Edwards (Cactus)

131. "Three Piece Suit"—Trinity (Belmont)
132. "Tradition"—Trinity (Prophets)
133. "Tribal War"—Trinity (Nationwide)
134. "Tricked"—Ansel and the Meditations (Bam Bam)
135. "Two Sevens Clash"—Culture (Joe Gibbs)
136. "Under Heavy Manners"—Derrick Morgan (Justice)
137. "Unitone Skank"—Dr. Alimantado (Ital)
138. "Universal Natty"—I-Roy (Well Charge)
139. "War in the City"—Bob Andy (Jamrock)
140. "War ina Babylon"—Max Romeo (Island)
141. "We a Socialists"—The Youths (Youth Man)
142. "We Should Be in Angola"—Pablo Moses (Penetrate)
143. "Weeping"—Junior Byles (Thing)
144. "Whip Them Jah"—Dennis Brown (Flames)
145. "Who Has Eyes to See"—Errol Holt (Cry Tuff)
146. "Wolf and Leopards"—Dennis Brown (Observer)
147. "Words of the Prophet"—Trinity (Prophet)
148. "You're So Cold"—Tyrone Evans (Clocktower)
149. "The Youth"—Burning Spear (Spear)
150. "Zion Call"—Prince Far I (Cry Tuff)

APPENDIX B: 150 SONGS WE FORGOT TO MENTION

1. "1865 (96 Degrees in the Shade)"—Third World (1977)
2. "A Ju Ju Wah"—Prince Roland Downer and Count Ossie with His Band (1970)
3. "African Pose"—Anthony B and Famous Face (2011)
4. "Al Capone's Guns Don't Argue"—Dennis Alcapone (1971)
5. "All the Style"—Elephant Man (2003)
6. "And You Be Loved"—Damien "Jr. Gong" Marley (2001)
7. "Are You Going to Marry Me?"—Derrick and Patsy (1962)
8. "Bangarang"—Horace Andy (1988)
9. "Bankrobber"—Audioweb (1996)
10. "Beautiful Girls"—Sizzla (2007)
11. "Best Dressed Chicken in Town"—Dr. Alimantado (1978)
12. "Billie Jean"—Shinehead (1994)
13. "Black Star Liner"—Fred Locks (1976)
14. "Blind to You"—Collie Buddz (2008)
15. "Bloody Sunday"—Gentleman (2007)
16. "Boogie Rock"—Laurel Aitken (1960)
17. "Boom Shack-A-Lak"—Apache Indian (1993)
18. "Boombastic"—Shaggy (1995)
19. "Bye Bye Baby"—Dubwiser (1997)
20. "Children"—Yami Bolo (2000)
21. "Clarks"—Vybz Kartel (2010)
22. "Coca Cola Shape"—Sasha (2005)
23. "Cockney Translation"—Smiley Culture (1982)
24. "Come Over"—Estelle and Sean Paul (2009)

25. "Conquering Lion"—Vivian Jackson and the Ralph Brothers AKA Yabby You (1972)
26. "Cool Meditation"—Third World (1979)
27. "Corrupted Thinkers"—Red Rose (2002)
28. "Dat"—Pluto Shervington (1976)
29. "Dog Your Woman"—Patsy and Peggy (1970)
30. "Don't Stroke My Pussy"—Katina (1972)
31. "Door Peep"—Burning Spear (1973)
32. "Download Million Stylez"—Ya Habibti (2011)
33. "Drive Me Crazy"—Richie Loop (2011)
34. "Dub B Good to Me"—Beats International (1990)
35. "Dub It inna Dance"—Ranking Joe (1980)
36. "East of the River Nile"—Augustus Pablo (1971)
37. "Easy Snapping"—Theo Beckford (1960)
38. "Everybody Needs Love"—Slim Smith (1969)
39. "Everything I Own"—Ken Boothe (1974)
40. "False Prophet"—Dennis Alcapone (1970)
41. "Fat Man"—Derrick Morgan (1960)
42. "Fire in Your Wire"—Patsy (1968)
43. "Flesh of My Skin"—Keith Hudson (1975)
44. "Forty Supem"—Capleton (2006)
45. "Furnace"—Keith Hudson (1972)
46. "Ganja Farmer"—George Dekker (2006)
47. "Girlie Girlie"—Sophia George (1985)
48. "Good Thing Going"—Sugar Minott (1981)
49. "Greetings"—Half Pint (1985)
50. "Have You Ever"—Andy and Joey (1962)
51. "Heads High"—Mr. Vegas (1998)
52. "Hello Stranger"—Brown Sugar (1977)
53. "Hold Yuh"—Gyptian (2010)
54. "Housewife's Choice"—Derrick and Patsy (1962)
55. "How Am I"—Mikey Spice (2000)
56. "I'm with the Girls"—Sizzla (2005)
57. "Jenny Lee"—Owen Gray (1960)
58. "Judgement Day"—Laurel Aitken (1960)
59. "Jungle Walk"—Dandy Livingstone (1968)

60. "Killer Man Jaro"—Dillinger (1976)
61. "King of the Dancehall"—Beenie Man (2005)
62. "Know Fari"—Bongo Herman and Eric "Bingy Bunny" Lamont (1971)
63. "Know How You Stand"—Dadawah (1974)
64. "Ku Klux Klan"—Steel Pulse (1978)
65. "Leave Earth"—Derrick Morgan (1961)
66. "Leggo Skanga"—Rupie Edwards (1975)
67. "Let's Get It On"—Shabba Ranks (1995)
68. "Live the Life You Love"—Mikey General (2004)
69. "Living on the Front Line"—Eddy Grant (1979)
70. "Longing For"—Jah Cure (2005)
71. "Love Has Found Its Way"—Dennis Brown (1982)
72. "The Love of Jah"—Mikey General (2001)
73. "Love of the Common People"—Nicky Thomas (1970)
74. "Mad About You"—Bruce Ruffin (1972)
75. "Make It Clap"—Busta Rhymes featuring Sean Paul (2003)
76. "Marcus Garvey"—Burning Spear (1975)
77. "Marijuana in My Brain"—Dillinger (1979)
78. "Mash! Mr. Lee"—Byron Lee and his Dragonaires (1961)
79. "Miss Fatty"—Million Stylez (2009)
80. "The Mission"—Stephen and Damien Marley (2008)
81. "Move Up (Nyah Bongo)"—Al and the Vibrators with Count Ossie and His Band (1967)
82. "Mr. Loverman"—Shabba Ranks (featuring Chevelle Franklyn) (1992)
83. "Mr. Policeman"—Busty and Cool (1962)
84. "Murder She Wrote"—Chaka Demus and Pliers (1994)
85. "Musical Drum Sound"—I-Roy (1972)
86. "My Conversation"—The Uniques
87. "Nah Give Up"—Gipsy King (2001)
88. "Nah Run from It"—Princess and Sister Wendy (1995)
89. "Nicer by the Hour"—Rocker-T (2000)
90. "Now That We've Found Love"—Third World (1978)
91. "Oh Carolina"—Shaggy (1993)
92. "OK Fred"—Errol Dunkley (1979)

93. "Open the Door"—Clive and Naomi (1965)
94. "Or Wah"—Capleton (2005)
95. "The Plane Land"—Richie Spice (2008)
96. "Pon di Corner"—Anthony B (2001)
97. "Prodigal Son"—Steel Pulse (1978)
98. "Punani fi Smell"—Gospel Fish (1991)
99. "Pussy Price Gone Up"—Laurel Aitken (1969)
100. "Rasta Communication"—Keith Hudson (1978)
101. "Ready for the Dancehall Tonight"—Peter Bouncer (1988)
102. "Real Killa"—Bounty Killer (2003)
103. "Rightful Ruler"—Paul Hue and Alkachaz (2001)
104. "Rise Jah Jah Children"—Ras Michael and the Sons of Negus (1974)
105. "River Jordan"—Clancy Eccles (1961)
106. "Rivers of Babylon"—Prince Student (1972)
107. "Rock Me Baby"—Brenda Jones (1996)
108. "Rockers Galore"—Mikey Dread (1981)
109. "Rough Rider"—Lloydie and the Lowbites (1970)
110. "Rub Up Push Up"—The Termites (1968)
111. "Rude Boy Ska"—Lionrock (1998)
112. "S90 Skank"—Big Youth (1972)
113. "Satchmo's Mash Potato"—Girl Satchmo (1961)
114. "Satta Massagana"—The Abyssinians (1968)
115. "Screaming Target"—Big Youth (1973)
116. "Searching"—China Black (1994)
117. "Sex Grand National"—Matador and Fay (1973)
118. "Shake a Leg"—Derrick Morgan (1961)
119. "Shanky Dog"—Bunny Flip (1972)
120. "Sideshow"—Barry Biggs (1976)
121. "Silly Games"—Janet Kay (1979)
122. "Sit Down and Cry"—Errol Dunkley (1980)
123. "Smoking"—Keith Hudson (1976)
124. "Sound System"—Steel Pulse (1979)
125. "Stop the Abuse"—Desperado (2003)
126. "Straight Up!"—Sean Paul (2005)
127. "Sweets for My Sweet"—C. J. Lewis (1994)

128. "Tek Weh Yuh Self"—Mr. Vegas (2009)
129. "Telephone Love"—J. C. Lodge (1990)
130. "Tell Dem"—Hi Fi Killers (1998)
131. "Time to Shine"—Nemesis (2007)
132. "Tree of Life"—President Brown (2004)
133. "Try If You Want"—Beres Hammond (2006)
134. "Untold Stories"—Buju Banton (1995)
135. "Uptown Top Ranking"—Althea and Donna (1977)
136. "Wa Do Dem"—Eek-A-Mouse (1981)
137. "Walking Down King Street"—Theo Beckford (1962)
138. "Want a Grine"—Melinda Slack and Lee Perry (1974)
139. "Warrior Love"—Etana (2008)
140. "We Be Burnin'"—Sean Paul (2005)
141. "What a Gwaan"—Cutty Ranks (2003)
142. "What's Going On"—Spanner Banner featuring Trouble (2002)
143. "Who Am I"—Beenie Man (1998)
144. "Who Win di War"—Shabba Ranks (2012)
145. "Wine Gyal"—Beenie Man (2008)
146. "Woman a Come"—Marguerita (1964)
147. "Words of Wisdom"—Max Romeo (1972)
148. "World Gone Crazy"—Dub Pistols featuring Horace Andy (2001)
149. "Yamaha Skank"—Rupie Edwards (1973)
150. "Zungguzungguguzungguzeng"—Yellowman (1983)

APPENDIX C: 100 ALBUMS YOU MUST HEAR

1. The Abyssinians: *Forward onto Zion* (Different, 1976)
2. The Abyssinians and Friends: *The Tree of Satta, Volume One* (Blood and Fire, 2004)
3. Althea and Donna: *Uptown Top Ranking* (Front Line, 1978)
4. Horace Andy: *Good Vibes* (Blood and Fire, 1997)
5. Horace Andy: *In the Light/In the Light Dub* (Blood and Fire, 1995)
6. Buju Banton: *Unchained Spirit* (Anti, 2000)
7. Big Youth: *Natty Universal Dread, 1973–1979* (Blood and Fire, 2001)
8. Big Youth: *Reggae Phenomenon* (Negusa Nagast—JA, 1974)
9. Big Youth: *Dreadlocks Dread* (Front Line, 1978)
10. Black Uhuru: *Showcase* (Front Line, 1981)
11. Black Uhuru: *Sinsemilla* (Island, 1981)
12. Annette Brissett: *Name of Life* (JVC, 2002)
13. Dennis Brown: *The Promised Land, 1977–1979* (Blood and Fire, 2002)
14. Burning Spear: *Marcus Garvey* (Island, 1975)
15. Junior Byles: *Beat Down Babylon* (Trojan—U.K., 1973)
16. Junior Byles and Friends: *129 Beat Street: Ja-Man Special, 75–78* (Blood and Fire, 1998)
17. Cornell Campbell: *I Shall Not Remove, 1975–80* (Blood and Fire, 2000)
18. The Chantells and Friends: *Children of Jah, 1977–1979* (Blood and Fire, 1999)

19. Chaka Demus and Pliers: *All She Wrote* (Mango, 1994)
20. Johnny Clarke: *Dreader Dread, 1976–1978* (Blood and Fire, 1998)
21. Johnny Clarke: *Rockers Time Now* (Virgin, 1976)
22. Jimmy Cliff: *Hard Road to Travel* (Island, 1968)
23. Jimmy Cliff: *Rebirth* (Hellcat, 2012)
24. Jimmy Cliff et al: *The Harder They Come—Original Soundtrack* (Island, 1972)
25. The Congos: *Heart of the Congos* (Blood and Fire, 1996)
26. The Congos and Friends: *Fisherman Style* (Blood and Fire, 2006)
27. Culture: *Two Sevens Clash* (Joe Gibbs, 1977)
28. Desmond Dekker: *007 (Shanty Town)* (Beverley's, 1967)
29. Junior Delgado: *Ragamuffin Year* (Island, 1986)
30. Dillinger: *CB 200* (Island, 1976)
31. Dr. Alimantado: *House of Singles* (Greensleeves, 2006)
32. Rupie Edwards: *Ire Feelings: Chapter and Version* (Trojan, 1990)
33. The Gladiators: *Proverbial Reggae* (Front Line, 1978)
34. Niney Holness: *Blood and Fire 1971–72* (Trojan, 1988)
35. Niney Holness: *Dubbing with the Observer* (Trojan, 1975)
36. Keith Hudson: *Pick a Dub* (Blood and Fire, 1994)
37. Keith Hudson: *Rasta Communication* (Greensleeves, 1979)
38. Keith Hudson: *Too Expensive* (Virgin, 1976)
39. Gregory Isaacs: *Mr. Isaacs* (Blood and Fire, 2001)
40. I-Roy: *Don't Check Me with No Lightweight Stuff (1972–1975)* (Blood and Fire, 1997)
41. I-Roy: *Ten Commandments* (Front Line, 1977)
42. King Tubby and Friends: *Dub Gone Crazy* (Blood and Fire, 1994)
43. Luciano: *The Messenger* (Xterminator, 1996)
44. Damien Marley: *Welcome to Jamrock* (Universal, 2005)
45. Ziggy Marley and the Melody Makers: *Conscious Party* (Virgin, 1988)
46. The Maytals: *Funky Kingston* (Dragon, 1973)
47. The Maytals: *Reggae Got Soul* (Mango, 1976)
48. The Mighty Diamonds: *Ice on Fire* (1977)
49. Sugar Minott: *Herbman Hustling* (Black Roots, 1984)

50. Hugh Mundell: *Africa Must Be Free by 1983* (Message, 1978)
51. Junior Murvin: *Police and Thieves* (Island, 1976)
52. Johnny Osbourne: *Truth and Rights* (Studio One, 1979)
53. Sean Paul: *Dutty Rock* (VP, 2002)
54. Lee Perry: *Clint Eastwood* (Pama, 1969)
55. Lee Perry: *Return of the Super Ape* (Lion of Judah, 1978)
56. Lee Perry: *Super Ape* (Island, 1976)
57. Poet and the Roots: *Dread Beat an' Blood* (Front Line, 1978)
58. Prince Buster: *Dance Cleopatra* (Prince Buster, 1970)
59. Prince Buster: *Fabulous Greatest Hits* (Fab, 1967)
60. Prince Far I: *Silver and Gold, 1973–1979* (Blood and Fire, 2005)
61. Prince Far I: *Under Heavy Manners* (Joe Gibbs, 1977)
62. Prince Far I: *Message from the King* (Front Line, 1978)
63. Shabba Ranks: *X-tra Naked* (Sony, 1992)
64. The Revolutionaries: *Vital Dub* (Virgin, 1976)
65. Max Romeo: *Let the Power Fall* (Dynamic, 1972)
66. Max Romeo: *Open the Iron Gate, 1973–1977* (Blood and Fire, 1999)
67. Max Romeo: *War ina Babylon* (Island, 1976)
68. Garnett Silk: *It's Growing* (VP, 1992)
69. The Skatalites: *African Roots* (UA, 1978)
70. Leroy Smart: *Ballistic Affair* (Channel One, 1977)
71. Linval Thompson: *Ride On Dreadlocks, 1975–77* (Blood and Fire, 2000)
72. Peter Tosh: *Equal Rights* (Virgin, 1977)
73. Peter Tosh: *Legalise It* (Virgin, 1976)
74. Peter Tosh: *Live at the One Love Peace Concert* (JAD, 2000)
75. The Twinkle Brothers: *Love* (Virgin, 1979)
76. Trinity: *Shanty Town Determination* (Blood and Fire, 2000)
77. U-Brown: *Train to Zion* (Blood and Fire, 1997)
78. U-Roy: *Dread in a Babylon* (Virgin, 1975)
79. various: *1959–64: The Ska's the Limit* (Island, 1997)
80. various: *Club Reggae*, volumes 1–6 (Trojan, 1971–1974)
81. various: *The Complete UK Upsetter Singles Collection*, volumes 1–4 (Trojan, 1998–2001)
82. various: *Countryman* (Island, 1982)

83. various: *Rockers* (Island, 1979)
84. various: *The Dreads at King Tubby's—If Deejay Was Your Trade* (Blood and Fire, 1994)
85. various: *Tighten Up*, volumes 1–10 (Trojan, 1969–1973)
86. various: *Trojan 12-Inch Box Set* (2003)
87. various: *Trojan British Reggae Box Set* (2003)
88. various: *Trojan DJ Box Set* (2002)
89. various: *Trojan Lovers Box Set* (1999)
90. various: *Trojan Motor City Box Set* (2006)
91. various: *Trojan Rocksteady Box Set* (2002)
92. various: *Trojan Rude Boy Box Set* (2002)
93. various: *Trojan Skinhead Reggae Box Set* (2002)
94. Wailing Souls: *All Over the World* (Chaos, 1992)
95. Sylford Walker and Welton Irie: *Lamb's Bread International* (Blood and Fire, 2000)
96. Willi Williams: *Messenger Man* (Blood and Fire, 2005)
97. Yabby You: *Dub It to the Top, 1976–1979* (Blood and Fire, 2002)
98. Yabby You: *Jesus Dread* (Blood and Fire, 1997)
99. Tappa Zukie: *Tappa Zukie in Dub* (Blood and Fire, 1995)
100. Tappa Zukie: *MPLA* (Klik, 1976)

RECOMMENDED READING

Bass Culture: When Reggae Was King by Lloyd Bradley (Penguin, 2001)

Born fi' Dead by Laurie Gunst (Canongate Books, 2003)

Chanting Down Babylon—The Rastafarian Reader by Nathaniel Samuel Murrell, William D. Spencer, and Adrian Anthony McFarlane (Temple University Press, 1998)

DanceHall: From Slave Ship to Ghetto by Sonjah Stanley Niaah (University of Ottawa Press, 2010)

Dead Yard: A Story of Modern Jamaica by Ian Thomson (Nation Books, 2011)

Dub: Soundscapes and Shattered Songs in Jamaican Reggae by Michael Veal (Wesleyan Press, 2007)

Jamaican Folk Tales and Oral Histories by Laura Tanna (DLT Associates, Inc., 2000)

Kingston Noir edited by Colin Channing (Akashic, 2012)

The Rastafarians: Twentieth Anniversary Edition by Leonard E. Barrett (Beacon Press, 1997)

Wake the Town and Tell the People: Dancehall Culture in Jamaica by Norman C. Stolzoff (Duke University Press, 2000)

INDEX

If You Like Series

The If You Like series plays the game of cultural connectivity at a high level—each book is written by an expert in the field and travels far beyond the expected, unearthing treats that will enlighten even the most jaded couch potato or pop culture vulture.

If You Like the Beatles...

Here Are Over 200 Bands, Films, Records, and Other Oddities That You Will Love

by Bruce Pollock
Backbeat Books
978-1-61713-018-2 • $14.99

If You Like Metallica...

Here Are Over 200 Bands, CDs, Movies, and Other Oddities That You Will Love

by Mike McPadden
Backbeat Books
978-1-61713-038-0 • $14.99

If You Like Monty Python...

Here Are Over 200 Movies, TV Shows, and Other Oddities That You Will Love

by Zack Handlen
Limelight Editions
978-0-87910-393-4 • $14.99

If You Like The Terminator...

Here Are Over 200 Movies, TV Shows, and Other Oddities That You Will Love

by Scott Von Doviak
Limelight Editions
978-0-87910-397-2 • $14.99

If You Like The Sopranos...

Here Are Over 150 Movies, TV Shows, and Other Oddities That You Will Love

by Leonard Pierce
Limelight Editions
978-0-87910-390-3 • $14.99

If You Like Led Zeppelin...

Here Are Over 200 Bands, Films, Records, and Other Oddities That You Will Love

by Dave Thompson
Backbeat Books
978-1-61713-085-4 • $16.99

If You Like Quentin Tarantino...

Here Are Over 200 Films, TV Shows, and Other Oddities That You Will Love

by Katherine Rife
Limelight Editions
978-0-87910-399-6 • $16.99

If You Like Bob Marley...

Here Are Over 200 Bands CDs, Films, and Other Oddities That You Will Love

by Dave Thompson
Backbeat Books
978-1-4768-8681-7 • $16.99

If You Like True Blood...

Here Are Over 200 Films, TV Shows, and Other Oddities That You Will Love

by Dave Thompson
Limelight Editions
978-0-87910-811-3 • $16.99

Prices, contents, and availability subject to change without notice.

0213